"*The Year of Small Things* is the best kind of spiritual formation book: serious and funny, smart and vulnerable—and, most useful of all, practical. If you want to live the way of Jesus but struggle to know how to do this in the midst of family busyness, financial struggle, even depression, Sarah Arthur and Erin Wasinger can be trusted to help you and your community reimagine and engage in practices of spiritual wholeness and social justice. Honestly, this is one of my favorite books this year."

—**Jen Pollock Michel**, speaker and author
of *Teach Us to Want*

"This is the most provocative and profound book I've read in a long time. I plan to buy a box and give it to my friends so they can laugh, cry, repent, and soul-search as much as I did. Deeply moving—and necessary—for the faith community."

—**Joel Salatin**, renegade farmer and author
of *The Marvelous Pigness of Pigs: Respecting
and Caring for All God's Creation*

"Sarah Arthur and Erin Wasinger's beautiful book offers a minirevolution that could shake up the world, or at least your neighborhood—and it doesn't require growing kale or living in a hut. It begins with dinner. Open doors. Being real with one another. In a me-and-my-family-first culture, Arthur and Wasinger compellingly show us not only how we can *be* the body of Christ but how to actually *share life together* as the body of Christ."

—**Leslie Leyland Fields**, author of *Crossing the Waters:
Following Jesus through the Storms, the Fish,
the Doubt, and the Seas*

"*The Year of Small Things* is a field guide on how to implement Mother Teresa's admonition to 'do small things with great love.' In the midst of flu shots for the kids and complaints from the neighbors about the dandelions in the yard, the book shows—with abundant humor and grace—how to live a joyful, costly, and authentic faith."

—**Tim Otto**, copastor of the new monastic community
Church of the Sojourners in San Francisco,
author of *Oriented to Faith*, and coauthor of *Inhabiting the Church: Biblical Wisdom for a New Monasticism*

"I am often asked if intentional community is a short-lived fad for young, idealistic singles. I always respond that following a common set of spiritual practices for the sake of our neighbors is the basic lifestyle of a disciple. We then have a conversation about how 'realistic' it is to follow Jesus. Now I can refer them to *The Year of Small Things* as evidence of how some families with young children are in fact practicing intentional community in their suburban context. This beautifully written book is a gem!"

—**Elaine Heath**, dean of Duke Divinity School;
author of *God Unbound: Wisdom from Galatians
for the Anxious Church*

"What a wonderful story of two ordinary families dealing with the normal struggles of life, coming together to grow deeper in life with God. Written with grace, authenticity, and wit, Arthur and Wasinger's book made me excited to follow their path—the mark of a truly great work."

—**Nathan Foster**, director of community life, Renovaré;
author of *The Making of an Ordinary Saint*

"Sarah and Erin get it. They cut grapes for tiny fingers, they wipe runny little noses, they bandage skinned knees, and they love the world that God loves. If you want to practice your faith right where you are, these women are the reliable guides you need."

—**Margot Starbuck**, author of *Small Things with Great Love:
Adventures in Loving Your Neighbor*

the year of small things

Other Books by Sarah Arthur

The God-Hungry Imagination:
The Art of Storytelling for Postmodern Youth Ministry

Light upon Light:
A Literary Guide to Prayer for Advent, Christmas, and Epiphany

Between Midnight and Dawn:
A Literary Guide to Prayer for Lent, Holy Week, and Eastertide

Mommy Time: 90 Devotions for New Moms

The One Year Coffee with God

At the Still Point:
A Literary Guide to Prayer in Ordinary Time

the year of small things

radical faith for the rest of us

sarah arthur and erin f. wasinger

foreword by jonathan wilson-hartgrove

BrazosPress

a division of Baker Publishing Group
Grand Rapids, Michigan

Published by Brazos Press
a division of Baker Publishing Group
P.O. Box 6287, Grand Rapids, MI 49516-6287
www.brazospress.com

Printed in the United States of America

Library of Congress Cataloging-in-Publication Data
Names: Arthur, Sarah, author.
Title: The year of small things : radical faith for the rest of us / Sarah Arthur and
    Erin F. Wasinger.
Description: Grand Rapids : Brazos Press, 2017. | Includes bibliographical
    references.
Identifiers: LCCN 2016043393 | ISBN 9781587433825 (pbk.)
Subjects: LCSH: Families—Religious life. | Christian life.
Classification: LCC BV4526.3 .A78 2017 | DDC 248.4—dc23
LC record available at https://lccn.loc.gov/2016043393

17 18 19 20 21 22 23   7 6 5 4 3 2 1

For my husband, Tom,
our pietist in residence,
who practices more spiritual disciplines
with his pinky finger in ten minutes
than I do all week. Love you.
—Sarah

For Dave, who keeps saying yes.
—Erin

And for our beloved community
at Sycamore Creek Church,
which has taught us more
in these past twelve months
than we could ever hope
to learn on our own.

contents

acknowledgments

To paraphrase the now-famous acknowledgments in Brendan Pietsch's *Dispensational Modernism*, "We blame all of you." Writing this book has been something like running a marathon (Erin knows the running thing): we set out thinking it would be a worthy endeavor, a lifelong goal to check off, only to realize partway through that it might possibly kill us. But we survived thanks to loving spouses who ran with us, parents and friends who watched our children, Bob Hosack and the team at Brazos, and our church family that relentlessly prayed us to the finish line. We also couldn't have gone far without the guidance, prayer, and feedback of readers and advisors Amey Victoria Adkins, David Arthur and Rebecca Byrd, Chanequa Walker-Barnes, Rob Cook, Liz DeGaynor, Barb Flory, Elaine Heath, Aleah Marsden, Nathan Foster, Tim Otto, Margot Starbuck, Alice Fleming Townley, and a host of others. Whoever first established the hermitages at the De Sales Center— the writerly equivalent of hydration stations—*God bless you*. We did not perish. But there were lots of times we blamed you all for being so darn encouraging.

From Sarah: Many thanks to my patient husband, Tom, and our two little boys, Micah and Sam, who are now conditioned to feel abandonment whenever I open my laptop. Mommy is all done now, I promise. Thanks to my parents, Bob and Peg Faulman, who inevitably catch whatever diseases my children carry but lovingly watch them anyway. David and Penny Van Dam, your sweet lakefront "Mobe" was a lifesaver, the ultimate writer's retreat. Extra-special thanks to our church "grandma," Alice McKinstry, who had never heard of new monasticism but babysat my children, took them to play music at a nursing home with church friends from the neighboring trailer park, folded our laundry, welcomed struggling people to live in her house, loaned us her car, worked our soil, and bathed us in the love of Jesus—all so I could write a book about sharing life in the small things. Really, your name should be on the front cover, not mine. Finally, Erin, Dave, Alice, Violet, and Louisa, you are a treasure. I still can't believe you agreed to this. Here's to another year of small things!

From Erin: First, my love to Alice, Violet, and Louisa; may you continue to be curious, compassionate, and open to adventure. A million thank-yous to my parents, Phyllis and Bernie, who cheerfully asked to host the girls for long weekends so I could write. Jana Aupperlee, Barb Flory, Nancy Kingsley, Kristin Kratky, Jen Newman, and Emily Vliek—your grace and discernment with us were gifts. I'm ever grateful for the chance to tell and hear stories with Mrs. H's class at Mt. Hope STEAM School; thanks for sharing your Friday afternoons with me. *Merci beaucoup*, Sarah, Tom, Micah, and Sam; thanks for the invitation to change just about everything in our lives. "Small things," you said. "It'll be fun," you said. (We love you.) To Water City and Sycamore Creek churches: may you be blessed as you've both blessed our family. And Dave, always. I'd choose you again and again.

foreword

jonathan wilson-hartgrove

In the summer of 2016, when I first read this book, Simone Biles went to the Olympics in Rio and dazzled the world with her grace and skill as a gymnast. My daughter was six, and we happened to be spending the week at a beachside cottage that had been gifted to us. Every evening, after playing in the sand all day, we turned on the TV to watch the best gymnasts in the world—maybe the best of all time—and went to sleep in awe of what the human body can do.

Now my wife and I are trying to figure out how to get our daughter into gymnastics.

I suspect we're not alone. Watch any baby grow up and you learn that imitation is fundamental to human development. We imagine our own lives based on what we've seen and heard in the lives of others. Whenever someone strives to reach the fullness of her own potential, other people notice. We don't simply admire Simone Biles because of what *she* can do. Each of us also has to ask, even if we couldn't possibly say it aloud, "I wonder if I might be able to do that too?"

When Saint Paul searches for a metaphor to help people imagine
the spiritual life, he often chooses the Olympic athlete. "Train
yourself to be godly," he writes to Timothy (1 Tim. 4:7 NIV), using
the same Greek word that was used to describe Olympic training.
To the Corinthians he writes that this is his own model: "I strike a
blow to my body and make it my slave so that after I have preached
to others, I myself will not be disqualified for the prize" (1 Cor.
9:27 NIV). In the language of the Letter to the Hebrews, all such
striving is an imitation of Christ himself: "For the joy set before
him he endured the cross, scorning its shame, and sat down at the
right hand of the throne of God" (Heb. 12:2 NIV).

Imitate me as I imitate Christ, the apostle says. When someone
in contemporary society fasts for forty days or gets up to pray in
the middle of the night or sells his possessions to give to the poor,
we worry about him. That kind of devotion seems extreme. But
such discipline for the sake of Olympic glory is not considered
masochism. When my daughter watched Simone Biles, it seemed
natural for her to want to become what she'd seen.

When we see the fullness of our own potential in someone else,
it only makes sense to do everything we can to pursue it.

One thousand six hundred years ago, in the desert of Upper
Egypt, monasticism was born as a movement to follow the way
of Jesus to the fullness of our potential as daughters and sons
of God. By most every account, Saint Anthony was the spiritual
gold-medal Olympian of ancient Egypt. So many people went out
into the wilderness to imitate his asceticism that his biographer,
the bishop of Alexandria, said, "The desert became a city."

I love the story Saint Jerome tells in his *Life of Paul the Hermit*
about how Anthony, in his nineties, had a vision of a man, someone
even further advanced on the way to holiness than he was, living
in a remote cave somewhere in the desert. Knowing that he had to
learn from this man, even without knowing where he was—even
if he died trying to find him—the nonagenarian Anthony set out
across the hot sand of Upper Egypt, trusting that God would show

him the way. (Ask yourself what you would do if you learned that your grandparent had decided to make such a pilgrimage.)

Of course God leads Anthony to Paul the Hermit. Standing at the door to his cave, the great Abba Anthony begs to come in and sit at the feet of this man no one has ever heard of. He even says that he'll have to lay down and die there if Paul doesn't grant him an audience. Opening the door with a wry smile, Paul asks, "Are you surprised that I didn't rush to greet you after you threatened to die on my doorstep?"

Yes, you're supposed to laugh. Because in the end, the joke is on each of us. Whenever we see someone living the life that's really life—that fullness of what we were made for—it only makes sense that we would want to imitate it. Jesus says it would make perfectly good sense for us to go and sell everything we have to buy the pearl of great price. So we give ourselves to imitation. We strive to follow the way that has been paved by those who've gone before us—Christ himself chief among them.

All of this is natural, and it is good. But in the end, the joke is on us because no amount of training and striving—no discipline or monasticism—guarantees that we will grow up into the fullness of him who fills everything. I love that Saint Anthony knew, even at the end of his life, that he still had so much to learn. I love that he was still willing to sacrifice everything to sit at the feet of one who could teach him. And I love that Paul laughed at him—that he helped him to laugh at himself because, amid all his striving, God had already done everything that was needed to make him perfect.

I love that old story about Abbas Anthony and Paul for the same reason I love this book. It takes seriously the work that is ours to do—and the reason it's worth doing in a world where we are so easily held captive to the patterns of death by principalities and powers. These spiritual mothers of American suburbia have heard the call to sell all and follow after Jesus. And they have not gone away sad.

They have, instead, like the ammas of old, given their attention to training for godliness in the small things of everyday life. Doing so, they have learned that this way is not easy—that it takes no less effort to live the way of Jesus in the suburbs than to live it in the inner city or the ancient desert. Reading their account, I see some ways that it's even harder. Wherever we are, it turns out, there is a cross to bear if we are willing.

But that is not all. At the end of the day, the joke is on them, just as the joke is on me. The joke is on each of us. I can see old Paul the Hermit smiling. I can hear Jesus saying to the disciples, "It is your Father's good pleasure to give you the kingdom" (Luke 12:32 ESV). I hear Abba Anthony whispering at the end of his life, "I no longer fear God, but I love him."

And I laugh. I laugh till I cry, just like I imagine Simone Biles must have when, after all those years of work, she nailed her routine, won the gold, and knew deep down inside that it was all a gift.

introduction

the street view

One of the elders said: Either fly as far as you can from
men, or else, laughing at the world and the men who
are in it, make yourself a fool in many things.
—Desert Fathers (4th c.)[1]

Sleeves rolled up on a gorgeous fall day last week, I (Sarah) grabbed
a rag from a bucket of soapy water and ran it along the hood of the
little car in my suburban driveway. It was not my car—you'll have
to wait till the end of the book to find out why that matters—but
I had offered to wash it. And it was not my house; this was the
parsonage to which my husband and I had been appointed when
he said yes to itinerant ministry. But it was our home. My two
little boys were napping, the leaves were turning, and warm sun
bathed my grubby sweatshirt and jeans as I cheerfully scrubbed a
decade's worth of bugs off the front grill. Children called to each
other in the nearby green space. Someone walked by and waved.
This is good, I thought, humming. Life is good.

1

And then a car drove by, one of those with a camera on top, the kind that takes pictures for online maps. It cruised down my cul-de-sac, went around the loop, and came back, making a leisurely turn past the parsonage. Three hundred and sixty degrees of street view, documenting the bucket, the soapy rag, the little car, the shop vac, my work clothes, the squint on my face as I stood in my suburban driveway, feeling a mixture of amusement and annoyance. I realized there would now be a public record that I do, in fact, live here—the last place I ever expected to call home. Presumably, anyone zooming in on our street would see a typical middle-class suburban woman doing a typical middle-class suburban task, washing a typical middle-class suburban car. What they would not see is the journey I'm still taking to be at peace with this, to live my faith on the ground in this context.

And they wouldn't know what the car *means*.

•••••

You see, this hasn't always been my zip code. Before moving here six years ago, my husband Tom and I lived for three years of graduate school in an intentional Christian community called Isaiah House of Hospitality located in northeast central Durham, North Carolina. This was effectively the inner city, one of America's abandoned places, complete with all the stereotypes: boarded-up houses, overgrown lawns, rusted cars, police tape, prostitutes, roaming dogs. FBI raids. Gunfire at night, especially in the summer. Drive-by shootings of children.

And yes, we lived there on purpose.

Well, to be exact, our housemates Rebecca Byrd and her husband, David Arthur (no relation to us), lived, and still live, there on purpose. In fact, they plan to raise their children, grow old, and die there. Smack in the middle of Police District No. 1, Durham's "bull's-eye" for the most known residences of gang members, they will continue to renovate that former crack house and work the quarter acre of urban garden and feed their chickens and take in the homeless. There where David once found a bullet lodged in the shingles of the front porch. There where Rebecca once told a fugitive hiding on the back porch, in the midst of a block-wide manhunt, "Children are in this house, and you will leave *right now*" (hospitality has its limits).

This is where David and Rebecca were planted, mere blocks from the congregation where Tom and I worshiped during our years at Duke Divinity School. Through that congregation we met them and eventually moved into the household.

My in-laws not-so-jokingly called Isaiah House the hippie commune. And in many ways they were right. Together with other members of the household, we shared our worldly goods (except our bank accounts and underwear—*eww*), worked the earth, welcomed the homeless, and practiced most of the twelve "marks" of the radical Christian movement known as new monasticism—more on that shortly. We ate and prayed daily with our housemates, rotated chores, and befriended our homeless guests. We watched children, cooked meals, and mopped the everlastingly dirty kitchen floor. We attended hearings, went to prayer vigils, cleaned up an empty lot. It was hard. It was amazing. It changed our lives.

But we knew it was temporary. Once we graduated from Duke, our United Methodist bishop would appoint Tom to serve a church somewhere in our home state of Michigan. Submission to the itinerant system of our denomination meant no control over our next zip code. And while we knew this could be anywhere, needless to say we were not prepared for the culture shock of an appointment to the suburbs of Lansing, Michigan.

When we first pulled up in the moving truck that Memorial Day six years ago, I was a bewildered mess. Don't get me wrong: we were grateful. Grateful that our bishop had understood Tom's desire to learn church-planting culture and assigned him as the second pastor of a young church-plant near one of our state's largest urban centers. Grateful that Sycamore Creek Church had already welcomed us with open arms on two previous visits. Grateful that the church had carefully and thoughtfully, on a shoestring budget, purchased this suburban parsonage for its new pastor to live in. These were people who already loved us, based on no merits of our own, because that's how God loves. They had already spent dozens, maybe hundreds of hours cleaning, painting, and dealing with all the stresses of new home ownership—by committee, no less. And now they had given up their Memorial Day celebrations to stand in the driveway, waving, as we made the final turn after thirty hours in that blessed truck.

"Welcome home!" they said.

That Memorial Day in Michigan we learned something. We learned that the love of Jesus transcends zip codes. It even transcends whatever "rules" or "marks" you seek to live by. That day, smiling, generous people gave up their holiday to unload our stuff, set up our house, feed us and all the workers, and pray with us— breathtaking hospitality to the stranger on a communal scale. Culture shock aside, I've never been given a spiritual community so instantly, without guile or pretense, people determined to love us despite our panicked expressions, boxes of crap, and occasional superior asides ("oh, we won't be using the dishwasher because [insert self-righteous moralizing about our former life in a 'radical' household, combined with barely informed commentary about the global water crisis and probably something else about sustainability here]"). Grace, pure and simple.

•••••

And yet.

And yet, steady formation in a way of life changes you, for better or worse. Six years into our appointment here, Tom and I knew that we had begun to capitulate to suburbia's vision of the good life: two nice cars, a weed-free lawn, two well-dressed and well-shod boys (Micah, age four; Sam, age one), a pantry full of premade foods, and little to no intentional interaction with those on society's fringes. We were insanely busy with work, parenting, and church commitments. We could have easily convinced most anyone that we had no margin to reinstate some of the practices of simplicity, sustainability, and hospitality that had once characterized our life in community. In my husband's words, "I feel like our values have been neutered." So was that it? Was that all we could say about our lives? "We were cool once, and now we're just 'normal'—in all the worst ways."

It wasn't enough. We couldn't settle for simply thinking of radical faith as something in our past, a fun hobby, something possible only for those carefree, kid-free graduate students who had packed up and moved into the inner city just because we could. We began to realize we had to *reclaim and live* the practices that had become core to our understanding of what it means to follow Jesus. We had to translate some of the practices of radical faith—things like simplicity, hospitality, sustainability, reconciliation, justice—right here, right now.

Because if we were struggling against the false vision that comfort, safety, wealth, material possessions, pleasure, and leisure can bring ultimate fulfillment, then most likely other Christians had to be struggling too.

Enter Erin, Dave, and their three little girls (Alice, age six; Violet, four; and Louisa, two).

The short version of a difficult, beautiful story that Erin will soon tell in more depth is this: Three years ago, Dave and Erin left their jobs at a newspaper in Oshkosh, Wisconsin, for Dave to work at a sister publication, the *Lansing State Journal*, here in the capital city. They found Sycamore Creek Church. And after they had attended our church for a while, we learned that they too earnestly desired to loosen their grip on the American Dream. (I mean, what sort of middle-class mother cashes in her 401[k] from the job she left on purpose, in order to pay off school debt, so she could be ready for what God wanted next?) They had been reading the more "radical" voices in American Christianity—Francis Chan, David Platt, Shane Claiborne, Jonathan Wilson-Hartgrove—as well as

activists such as Dorothy Day of the Catholic Worker Movement
(a side of Catholicism these former Catholics had never dreamed
existed). And all of that was compelling. But they felt like they
were stumbling their way forward, alone and weird. Like us.

So we had them over for dinner.

"What if," we began to brainstorm, "what if we read some
books together?"

We're geeks, so that sounded great. We talked about those evangelical megachurch pastors such as David Platt (*Radical: Taking
Back Your Faith from the American Dream*) and Francis Chan
(*Crazy Love*) who are calling God's people to eschew the American
Dream in favor of global missions.[2] We agreed that while they're
making some good points, our real roots and interests connect more
with the movement known as new monasticism, as expressed by
its chief spokespersons, Shane Claiborne (*The Irresistible Revolution*) and Jonathan Wilson-Hartgrove (*New Monasticism*; *God's
Economy*; *Strangers at My Door*). Described in broad brushstrokes,
new monastics are downwardly mobile, youngish adults from all
denominational backgrounds who form intentional Christian
households or communities in abandoned urban centers, and
who are identified by twelve unique marks—including simplicity,
hospitality, reconciliation, and contemplative Christian practices,
among others.

This was our (the Arthurs') background; these were our people.
Finding another couple willing to talk about this—who even knew
what new monasticism *meant*—was like finding people who speak
your mother tongue. And all this reading and discussing was great,
except . . . nothing had changed. At another dinner, in early summer, we wondered, "What if . . . what if we actually tried this
radical faith thing right here, right now? What if we made this
some kind of yearlong experiment?"

And that's when our imaginations began buzzing. What if we
took the twelve marks of new monasticism and attempted to
translate them into our context, one per month, over the course

of a year? We weren't trying to change the world here. In fact, the most we could probably manage was one small practice, one tiny change, in each area. But we could at least *try*. And best of all, we could hold one another accountable.

"I think this should be a book," I said to Erin that night. Dinner was over. All nine of us had emerged onto the parsonage lawn, where a warm, light rain pattered around us in the dusk. Our children twirled, giggling, while I yanked up rhubarb stalks and placed them in Erin's waiting arms. "I think," I said, "it should be called *The Year of Small Things*. And I want you to write it with me."

One look at Erin's face told me everything. "Yes!" she said, her face wet with rain—or was it tears? "*Yes!*"

That night we stood in the front yard, faces upturned to those watery clouds, realizing that a year of living radically was somehow bigger and yet more manageable than we could have dreamed— now that we had accountability. We were like the newly returned exiles in the Hebrew Scriptures: the deep thirst to restore the dream, the reclaimed vision of what could be after what had been. It was all possible. Hard, but possible.

"For whoever has despised the day of small things shall rejoice," wrote the prophet Zechariah when the people of God had begun to rebuild the temple (4:10). Yes, the new temple was tiny compared to the old. It lacked the former glory, the attraction, the bling. And the Israelites who remembered the first temple wept when they saw it (see Ezra 3:12). But the second was built out of obedience. It was built out of a desire to do the best with what they had, because small things for God were better than no things. And God promised to bless it (see Hag. 2:9).

Not all of us will move to the inner city or live with the homeless or protest unjust laws before city councils. Some of us will do just one of those things; a few of us might do several. But many of us are called to try this radical thing right where we are, facing our current battles and barriers, one day at a time. Mother Teresa is often quoted as saying, "We can do no great things, only small things with great love." Well, that's all we've got. Small changes, small acts of hospitality, small attempts at solidarity with "the least of these." This is what our families, with help from some wise friends and our local church, attempted over the course of one year, taking notes as we went. We hope that others, like you, will not only rejoice with us but give it a shot.

Welcome to the year of small things.

•••••

Before we go any further, what are the twelve marks of new monasticism? This is a good page to flag, because we'll be coming back to it a lot. First, the marks or practices are not "rules," although they were born out of a conversation back in 2004 between a number of communities that were practicing radical discipleship and considered establishing a kind of "rule of life," like the older monastic orders (such as the Benedictines and the Jesuits). They didn't end up establishing a "rule," but they did identify what appeared to be the key characteristics or practices of those communities. Taken all together, these practices become what new monastics call a "school for conversion," the training ground for turning one's life away from the false promises of the American Dream and toward Jesus.

❧ Twelve Marks of a New Monasticism

1. Relocation to the abandoned places of Empire.
2. Sharing economic resources with fellow community members and the needy among us.
3. Hospitality to the stranger.
4. Lament for racial divisions within the church and our communities combined with the active pursuit of a just reconciliation.

5. Humble submission to Christ's body, the church.
6. Intentional formation in the way of Christ and the rule of the community along the lines of the old novitiate.
7. Nurturing common life among members of intentional community.
8. Support for celibate singles alongside monogamous married couples and their children.
9. Geographical proximity to community members who share a common rule of life.
10. Care for the plot of God's earth given to us along with support of our local economies.
11. Peacemaking in the midst of violence and conflict resolution within communities along the lines of Matthew 18.
12. Commitment to a disciplined, contemplative life.[3]

During one of our earliest conversations about all this (if you can call it a conversation, since we spent most of the time refereeing small children), it became pretty clear that these twelve marks and our twelve months were not going to line up perfectly.

"I love this," Erin said. "But I don't quite get it. How do you do these things with small kids? Do you just add 'with children' to the end of each sentence? And anyway, are no women writing about new monasticism?"

"They're busy changing diapers," I said.

The questions kept piling up: What are we supposed to do about debt? Are celebrations allowed? How about Christmas presents? Can you hire a sitter so you can go on date night? And what about depression or other mental or physical illnesses? Is it selfish to take care of yourself, or can you get a gym membership? Is eating kale required (Erin asks warily, edging away)? And so on.

If we were going to tackle some of these issues—especially given our suburban (and in Erin and Dave's case, rural) context—we realized our twelve practices were not going to line up perfectly with new monasticism's twelve marks. In fact, discernment about what God wanted us to do, in our unique families, given our unique circumstances, would be the single most important Christian practice we would learn.

Meanwhile, as the year progressed, other concerns that affected our two families became evident, concerns that no doubt affect our readers as well.

First, privilege. There's no getting around the fact that our families are able to *choose* practices of downward mobility because of our cultural status as educated, white, middle-class Americans. This is one of those moments when the gospel, rather than comforting the afflicted (as the old saying goes), instead afflicts the comfortable. We're assuming that if you find the title of this book compelling, you're probably not among the afflicted. You may *feel* afflicted sometimes, particularly when it comes to debt, stress, or any number of first-world problems. But if the bottom falls out, you have a network of support that will keep you living at roughly the same level you do now. That's us too. Fair warning: things will get harder. Chapter 12 may not be your favorite.

Second, we recognize that yearlong experiments are a trend. While we were wrapping up the first drafts of this manuscript, the book *The Year without a Purchase* came out, chronicling one family's attempt to live more simply after serving as missionaries in Central America. It's hilarious and worth the read. We're not pretending to have invented anything new. However, the fact that we are a "we" and not an isolated individual or family is, we feel, significant. This entire project is born out of a covenantal friendship between families embedded within a worshiping congregation of people who are seeking, in small and big ways, to follow Jesus in solidarity with those who struggle. This is not a personal hobby that makes a great read when we're done. This is, in the language of new monasticism, a lifelong "school for conversion," in which we voluntarily engage in communal accountability to turn toward Christ *as a people* for the rest of our lives. If you're going to make lasting change, you need a posse. You need covenantal friendships. And some, if not many, of those friends need to be among the poor.

Third, we recognize that a growing number of counter-voices are responding to the more radical trends of American Christianity, including Jonathan Hollingsworth's poignant missionary memoir *Runaway Radical: A Young Man's Reckless Journey to Save the World.* We've shared some of our own cautions and questions in appendix A. But we want to be clear: we are not defending the suburbs. We believe that zip codes matter. When the new monastics claim as their first mark or practice "relocation to abandoned places of Empire," we take them seriously. In fact, partway through this experiment our entire *congregation* moved from worshiping in suburbia to buying a former Methodist church building smack in the middle of Lansing proper. This was huge. This was the single biggest thing that happened in this year of small things. And it changed the Wasingers—changed all of us —permanently.

But the parsonage didn't move. Tom and I remain in suburbia—because we also take the new monastics seriously when they insist on "humble submission to Christ's body, the church." In fact, the tension between these two marks lies at the heart of this experiment. And yet, no matter who we are or where we live, our current location doesn't give us a pass. If anything, the reality of zip code forces us to practice daily discernment about what, in fact, God is calling us to do, particularly when it comes to solidarity with the poor.

And therein lies the biggest challenge: discernment. Trying to figure out what God wants *you*, within the context of your church and community, to do. Perhaps you too have been reading and listening to some of the more radical voices in American Christianity, and perhaps you too have felt both convicted and confused about how to respond. In reading these voices it's easy to assume that, one, radical faith is nothing less than changing the whole world; and two, changing the world begins with those of us who call ourselves Christians becoming *more committed.*

Now, some of these guys attempt to clarify that it's about changing our own hearts, which is true. And it starts with one person at a time, which is also true. But it feels like the overarching message is that if we were *really, really dedicated* as followers of Jesus, if we really took Jesus seriously, there would be no global food crisis or sex trafficking or nuclear arms race or (insert your systemic sin of choice).

Which means we're all flunking. Big-time. As one commentator put it, "It's really hard to read these books, one after another, and confidently declare yourself a Christian at the end."[4] Even I feel like that, and I regularly invite the poor to live in my house. To my knowledge this has made zero impact on my city's housing problems, much less on global poverty. There is no village in sub-Saharan Africa that now has running water because of me—and I have lived in sub-Saharan Africa.

Not to diminish what so many amazing people are doing out there, the sacrifices they are making, the journeys God has called them on. Some of you *are* those people—or maybe *were*, having spent months or even years working for some mission agency or other, or living on purpose in the forgotten urban centers of America. But your own firebrand efforts have exhausted you. You became what you thought was really, really committed only to find yourself really, really burned out. Or maybe God called you to something else: graduate school, pastoral ministry in a small town, caring for a family member, getting married, having kids, getting out of debt, taking on a family business, battling illness, even battling post-traumatic stress disorder. And now you're feeling like a spiritual dropout, no longer really, really anything except tired.

Whether this call to downward mobility is new or you have done or are doing the radical thing, if you get nothing else out of this book, we want you to get this: radical faith is not about being übercommitted. It's not about being überspiritual. It's about *discernment.*

This isn't about receiving a sudden vision, a decided clarity about what you're supposed to do. Discernment is more like standing on a foggy mountain trail, peering into the gray mass that is your best guess at a trail. You take a few steps at a time, check your compass and the crumpled map in your pocket. Sometimes there's a surprise vista when the fog clears; occasionally you miss your turn. Most of the way you're plodding along without a clear sense of what's next. But you don't go it alone. You hike with a team. And together you listen for the voice of One calling in the fog.

One way we practice this listening is by sharing everyday life with others in covenantal friendship. And also by sharing everyday life with the stranger, the poor, the one with his "back against the wall."[5] Because when we share life, others' problems become our problems; the things God cares about become the things we care about. We discover turns on the trail that we never noticed on the map before. We witness a fellow hiker struggling, and we struggle too. And as a community we can leverage our strengths to bear one another's burdens.

That's how the world gets changed for the sake of Christ.

That's what radical faith looks like for the rest of us.

It's that small.

It's that huge.

•••••

So break it down: One city, one church, one year. Two families. Twelve small but radical changes. That's our story in a nutshell. That's what we'll be telling in this book: each chapter a different month, each month a different discipline, all cumulatively conspiring to make us a little less "normal," a lot more vulnerable, way more honest, and, we hope, a bit more like Jesus than we were last year.

What does this entail for you?

First, pick a month in which to start. For the Arthurs and the Wasingers, it was August 2014. We had been kicking around ideas since that rhubarb-picking epiphany in early summer, but finally we said, "Let's do this." For you (and your family, if applicable), it may be January, or it may be after school gets out. Whatever the case, pick a date. Say, "In two months, it's getting real around here." Say, "I don't fully get what this is about, but I know I need it." Say, "Let the wild rumpus begin!"

Then, make a list of practices. A glance at the covenant at the end of this introduction can be your guide. Each month we tackled a different area or topic in which to practice radical faith. Each family chose (or fell into) one small thing—just one—that we would begin to do in that area. Sometimes we chose the same thing. Sometimes our families each faced unique challenges that required unique focus. Whatever the case, we added those practices cumulatively over the course of the year, giving ourselves grace when we took more steps backward than forward, or when circumstances outside our control meant starting all over again, or when nothing seemed to be happening at all.

Don't worry: the twelve months are cumulative. You can go on to the next small thing even as you're working out the details of the previous ones. And you don't have to go in order (other than starting with covenantal friendship, which we feel is essential). It's all of a piece. Be patient with yourself. But start.

By the end of one year, where are you? Twelve steps closer, we hope, to the One who can make something out of nothing. You may not have changed the world, but you've begun to let God change you.

Below is the draft of our covenant, which details what we identified as each month's focus. This was not a slow warm-up: we dove right in. Tried and failed, tried again. Feel free to write your own version of what follows. Or simply read and reflect. In any case, pray. God may have different things in mind for you than God did for us. As we've said, the practice of discernment is the single most important spiritual discipline we learned along the way. This, we hope, will be the case for you as well.

Covenant

The year of small things: an experiment in small but radical changes, to embrace the way of Jesus, right where we are.

The challenge: to discern one small change in each of the following areas that we can embrace or reclaim over the course of the next year.

August: Covenantal Friendship

Through accountability and wisdom from others in intentional community, our first month is about covenanting in spiritual friendship with those who can help set the transparency and boundaries required for our yearlong experiment of small but radical changes.

September: Hospitality beyond Martha Stewart

Whether it's shared space (your home) or shared time (meals, laundry, holidays together), new monasticism is straightforward about welcoming the "other"—a radical reorientation of our culture's obsession with status and family, as well as an affront to our culture's distortions of true hospitality. We want to debunk the myth of "safety" and challenge all of us to welcome Christ in the stranger.

October: Radical Finances

Rejecting the American Dream. Period. (Debt reduction, spending less, giving more, accountability.)

November: Reclaiming Spiritual Habits

Reclaiming and integrating shared spiritual practices into our lives. (Prayer, confession, Sabbath, etc.)

December: Stuff
    Downsizing during the holidays; exploring what it means
    to be creators rather than consumers; navigating cultural
    and family expectations without "buying into" society's
    myth that stuff equals status or even love.

January: Holy Time
    Striking a balance between serving, working, family rela-
    tionships, creating, learning, personal health, social ob-
    ligations—not to mention friendship with the poor, the
    stranger, the other. In the new year, as busy families, how
    do we set apart Sabbath time?

February: Vows
    Strengthening our commitments in marriage or single-
    ness for the building up of the whole community and
    protecting those commitments when our culture—and
    even when all the good "radical" things we're attempting
    to do—overwhelms us.

March: Planted in the Church
    Recognizing that new monasticism is not a substitute for
    the local church; it isn't a new or alternative way of doing
    church but a unique "order" within the larger community of
    faith. Embedded in a local body of believers, we embrace the
    challenges and celebrate the victories of our congregation.

April: Kid Monasticism
    Shared life means not waiting till this season in our fami-
    lies' lives has passed or all our fears are addressed before
    we make radical changes. We affirm that our big decisions
    impact how our children participate in and experience
    God's kingdom. We encourage kids to grow in their faith
    and to serve God in radical ways too.

May: Sustaining Creation
Food choices, water conservation, community gardening, composting—we consider ways to live as sustainers of God's creation even as we recognize that it is creation, through God, that sustains us.

June: Unselfish Self-Care
It's at first a counterintuitive notion that to serve the community, you need to take care of yourself—and we don't see many new monastics discussing it, which is exactly why it needs to be talked about. How is taking care of yourself (your health, your exercise, your sleep, your diet, your downtime) a way of attending to the overall health of the community?

July: Just Living
To live in America means to participate in systems of injustice. But Christians cannot *just live*; rather, we must seek to *live justly*. So how can we as a worshiping community leverage our resources and our access to power—in solidarity with those who struggle—to make for change in this, God's city? We recognize with humility that we are going to mess this up. But we keep on.

Drafted in August 2014 by
Sarah, Tom, Micah, and Sam Arthur
Erin, Dave, Alice, Violet, and Louisa Wasinger

Reviewed by
David Arthur and Rebecca Byrd of Isaiah House of Hospitality, Durham, North Carolina

~~~~~ *Questions for Reflection and Discussion* ~~~~~~~~

1. If you could ask contemporary Christian radicals one question, what would it be?

2. Sarah and Erin talk a lot about the Christian practice of *discernment*, of seeing a way forward on the journey of faith *together with other Christians*. According to the apostle Paul in some of his letters to the early churches (see Eph. 1:17–19; Phil. 1:9–11; and Col. 1:9–10), how does discernment happen? What is the point?

3. How might your zip code affect your perceived ability to follow Christ in radical ways?

4. If you were to draft a covenant of twelve practices, what would it include? (For covenant suggestions and templates, see www.yearofsmallthings.com.)

~~~~~ *For Further Reading* ~~~~~~~~~~~~~~~~~~~

Claiborne, Shane. *The Irresistible Revolution: Living as an Ordinary Radical*. Grand Rapids: Zondervan, 2006.

The Rutba House, ed. *School(s) for Conversion: 12 Marks of a New Monasticism*. Eugene, OR: Cascade Books, 2005.

Starbuck, Margot. *Small Things with Great Love: Adventures in Loving Your Neighbor*. Downers Grove, IL: InterVarsity, 2011.

Thurman, Howard. *Jesus and the Disinherited*. 1949. Reprint, Boston: Beacon, 1996.

Wilson-Hartgrove, Jonathan. *New Monasticism: What It Has to Say to Today's Church*. Grand Rapids: Brazos, 2008.

1

covenantal friendship

Wait, you've heard of Shane Claiborne?
—Sarah Arthur (to Erin Wasinger, in one
of their first coherent conversations)

Sarah's Story

When Erin arrives with some ingredients for our weekly dinner, her three girls bundled against the cold, she looks tired and frazzled. At the last minute, Dave had to work the night shift. Because I'm deathly allergic to their dog, she is the one who comes to us. Even though it's six degrees and dropping. Even though she doesn't have winter boots. Even though it takes what feels like forty-seven minutes to get the girls suited up and out the door. Even though, as she will tell you, depression intensifies with the winter darkness and shutters her up inside like a caged animal. She is here, food in hand, ready to share a meal.

All because she and Dave made a vow of "yes" to this year of small things.

Dinner once a week. That's it. That's our one small thing in the quest to build community. We will attempt to do this again next week, although life regularly conspires to keep this from happening. If it's not soccer, it's travel, weather, or the never-ending flu season. When we first started, we managed it only monthly until Thanksgiving, then didn't pull it off again until late January. But it's always on the calendar. We're not going to beat ourselves up if it's not consistent. We figure hit or miss is better than never.

Erin shows up with Alice, Violet, and Louisa around 4:45, we pool what we've got in our pantries (usually coordinating ahead of time who will provide what), and we start to cook. Micah and Sam flail around in delirious excitement: so many blonde girls! Go crazy, Y chromosome! The children wander, fight, interrupt. Someone sets the table, arranges chairs. I attempt to ignore my dirty kitchen floor and hope the bathroom is at least serviceable. When not working the night shift, Dave shows up from work, pitches in. Tom pours some wine and goes on a problem-solving binge about the Wasingers' job situation or their housing quandaries. A child is pushed by another; there are tears.

We light a candle, say the opening verse of Psalm 23. We eat. The grown-ups talk. Reflect on this year of small things. How are finances going? Any breakthroughs on hospitality? Have you had a date night recently? Before I can finish a sentence—any sentence—Sam tips his bowl of risotto onto his tray, then onto himself. Occasionally we remember to invite the children to reflect on what Micah calls "instirring" questions. The children happily excuse themselves to play the fourteenth round of hide-and-seek. We talk until Sam or Louisa or both fall apart, then hurriedly clean up while the three oldest create a swirling vortex of tired craziness. We corral the troops, attempt to pray one last time by candlelight, sharing where we experienced God this week. It takes several adults to bundle everyone up, but before they leave we sing "Go Now in Peace."

Small things, we tell ourselves. Remember?

•••••

Covenantal friendship. That's the first task.

On the surface, it may sound rather simple: find a small group of other Christians (preferably local) who are interested in covenanting with you in shared practices of radical faith. People who will make vows to you, vows to lovingly ask you the hard questions.[1] But we'll be honest: this could be the hardest thing you do all year. It may be the first and only thing you truly flunk at.

That's because the quest for this kind of honest, vulnerable community flies in the face of rugged American individualism. The nuclear unit in the single-family home is the standard of our collective imagination. Most of us are raised by parents who have inherited this vision and attempted to make it happen, for better or worse. And once we get old enough, we are expected to forge our own way, start our own self-sufficient primary unit, complete with happy marriage, two kids, two cars, and, oh, let's throw in the picket fence.

But you and I know this isn't enough. It's not even working. As American demographics shift and our economic situation becomes more and more complex (read: difficult), it's clear that something needs to change. And rather than being the last to abandon the false promises of the American Dream, we as Christ-followers need to be at the front edge of something different. A new vision for sharing life. A vision of covenantal community.

So the year of small things begins here. It begins with a small group of fellow travelers on the journey, folks with whom we are vulnerable, folks who will hold us accountable, who are willing to share *life*, not just "outreach" or "mission." And by "life" we mean the material stuff of daily existence: the food, housing, transportation, chores, child care, prayers, conversations, finances, problem solving that it takes to make our lives run.

As I've already mentioned, when it comes to this aspect of radical faith, Tom and I have done some big things. While in seminary at Duke, we went from a one-bedroom apartment near campus (which we thought was small, after our house in northern Michigan) to *one bedroom* in Isaiah House. Shortly after we moved in, the residents of Isaiah House numbered twelve, including three nursing infants and a three-year-old. Yup. It was nuts.

Children cried at all hours of the day or night. Dinnertime was a crazy mash-up of vegetarian entrées, guests frying fish in what seemed like two feet of oil, and inedible-smelling baby food. The kitchen floor—mopped loyally once a week by Tom—stayed clean for the thirty seconds it took him to rinse out the mop. When seminary friends would ask us, "How's life in community going?" we'd say, "It's hard." But when they inevitably followed up with, "So are you going to leave?" we'd say, "What? No. This is where God has called us."

It was tough; it was also full of joy. We went on retreats to the mountains and the sea. We decorated for Advent, watched babies take their first steps, borrowed from and loaned things to our neighbors. We worshiped together at our local church. When Rebecca had their second son, we took turns hanging out with Big Brother till grandparents arrived.

Sharing life.

It was perhaps the closest I've ever come to the vision of community that we see in Acts 2:41–47. The passage depicts the strange result of Jesus's mandate to go into all the world (Matt. 28:19–20): a vision of people who stay put, doing life together. They hold all things in common, share resources, help others in the community who have needs, worship together, study, pray, break bread in one another's homes, and celebrate the God who makes it all possible. And not just occasionally, for special events like Easter, but "day after day." For weeks, months, years.

It's easy for Tom and me to judge our other attempts at building community against that radical experience. But this is not the year of big things; it's the year of small things. So the struggle for us is not to try and *replicate* Isaiah House in a new context but to discern what a creative reframing of that vision could look like.

•••••

The new monastics value both "nurturing common life" and "geographical proximity to community members," and it was in this spirit that we attempted to build some kind of community in our new suburban neighborhood. Our first few years in Lansing were like a gag reel of outtakes: one failed attempt after another. We started a community garden in our subdivision, which, after two summers of attrition in the volunteer pool as well as the addition of small children to our family, now lies abandoned by everyone except the birds and our neighbor who is forced to look at it from his kitchen window. We also attempted to share lawn-care equipment with another family down the street: they used our mower in the summer, and we used their snowblower in the winter—when it worked, which was almost never. The list goes on.

Eventually we figured out that the Wasingers happened to live roughly ten minutes down the road. Not just neighborly acquaintances, but genuine, on-the-ground, in the flesh potential partners in this radical Christian thing. Friends who were willing to ask us the tough questions—and who were willing to let us do the same for them. And so our challenge, as this year began, was not just to envision but actually to build community together.

What does "shared life" look like between separate households, separate schedules, separate finances? Both dads work outside the home in demanding jobs that often include evening responsibilities. Both women are write-at-home moms of small children, which at times feels like living under house arrest. Until recently Erin homeschooled their three girls; I arrange part-time child care for Sam so I can freelance while Micah is in preschool. Both families are deeply invested in ministry at our church, which involves meetings, billions of emails, planning, programs, Sunday-morning responsibilities, and billions of emails—did I say that already? Billions. Add errands, doctor's appointments, the occasional extra-curricular activity, plus eleven other intentional spiritual practices over the course of a year, and dinner together once a week feels downright heroic.

So we start there, and along the way we consider how to shoulder the burdens and blessings of hospitality. We trade, borrow, or give material things that the other family might need. We brainstorm child-care needs between the two households. We look at each other head-on and say, "So, how is it with your soul?"

Community on this scale is a not-so-subtle subversion of our culture's top value: take care of your own. Deal with what you need to deal with, but do so within your family unit. Rely on those people first, and if you haven't got family to speak of, either become some kind of burned-out attempt at a superhero or fill out an application for social services. Whatever you do, don't drag your "church family" into the mess, aside from the occasional prayer request (because, let's be honest, most of us don't really mean that phrase "church *family*"—not really). Rugged individualism, right?

Or, as Erin and Dave learned, *wrong*.

Erin's Story

"Whoa. I almost filed your email in the 'family' folder," Sarah told me over the phone the other day. We were discussing church programming details during Sam's naptime, which is one of the few times of day either of us can complete a sentence.

"Well, we kinda are now."

Around the Arthurs' dinner table, we had made vows to each other as friends. We had scribbled a covenant and ratified it with David and Rebecca of Isaiah House. We had tossed around the vague buzzwords "community" and "shared life," eventually zeroing in on "covenantal friendship." We promised to be transparent; we promised to be one another's cheerleaders. We didn't know then, of course, that we would come to love one another, but that happened too, somewhere along the way. We had become family.

Dave and I had needed this kind of friendship on a deep level. We'd tried the rugged individualism thing the first seven or eight years of our marriage, living eight hours from family.

We had three kids in rapid succession. We had two cars, a century-old story-and-a-half home in Wisconsin, and a dog named after a character from *Sex in the City*. We had the makings of the American Dream: the education, the full-time newspaper jobs, the marigolds in the landscaping. And the debt. Oh, the debt: our student loans, the car payments, the hospital bills. The picket-fence thing is all I thought I wanted.

Once I had it, though, my imagination froze. I remember those weeknights vividly. I'd set a glass of red wine beside me while I folded laundry in front of public television shows. Dave would come home long after I went to bed. A baby might stir upstairs, and I'd mourn that I got to see her only one hour that day. I might hear a car door slam, the neighbors coming home. I didn't know their names.

And then Dave started going to this little church that met in an old photography studio. Water City Church was so unlike the Catholicism we had grown up with. The pastor took the congregation on a five-year walk through the book of Matthew. They sang old hymns and David Crowder songs, and some would raise their arms in exultation, eyes closed. Unnerved, Dave and I sipped our beverages and observed for the first few months. Still, they welcomed us like old friends whenever we walked in. We began to share dinners, swap babysitting nights, and have long conversations over tea about careers and parenthood. I loved them before I knew I also loved Jesus.

Jesus bowled us over there in illustrations and metaphor. The Holy Spirit had ample time to hook us on that phrase Saint Matthew uses over and over: "the kingdom of heaven." "The kingdom of heaven is like," Pastor Jason would repeat and unpack, week after week: it's like a mustard seed, yeast, hidden treasure; it's like a wedding feast and bridesmaids waiting for the groom. Easy to enter for those who are humble as children, but difficult for the rich. Jesus's parables and Jason's teaching wove cross-grained with the growing sensation in my gut that Dave and I had to choose: Would we follow Jesus (whatever that meant), or would we let this feeling pass (maybe it was just indigestion)?

Spoiler alert: it was not indigestion. Matthew's Gospel unnerved us to the point of response. We began praying with the girls ("I think I'm doing it right," I told my friend Amy). We learned to tithe. We bought a children's Bible and read it at bedtime.

We started to wonder—aloud—if we ought to get serious about the debt thing, the career thing, the Jesus thing. A series of small yeses thawed our imaginations on what the kingdom of heaven might look like *now*—yes to helping lead the moms group at church, yes to taking communion there, yes to volunteering in Sunday school, yes to the refugee resettlement project. Questions bloomed in that fertile ground, and we got a bit ambitious: What *couldn't* we say yes to? Quitting the job that paid for day care? Moving to be closer to family in Ohio? Using our gifts and passions for the elusive yet all-encompassing kingdom of heaven?

The kingdom leaves no map, and all we had were a bucketful of parables and the energy that said we could do this (whatever "this" was). We had no plans, but when a job posted at a sister newspaper in Lansing, Michigan, Dave sent his résumé. Late in August 2012, Lansing called.

The five Wasingers—plus Mr. Big, the carsick mutt—piled into the van for a tour that lasted fewer than forty-eight hours of the city that could be home. As we left Oshkosh early on a Saturday morning, I saw a friend running on the bridge on Wisconsin Street. What a bizarre memory of her, one of the people I loved best, in the rearview mirror . . . like I was already saying good-bye.

"Welcome to Pure Michigan," a blue sign beckoned four or five hours later.

My heart skipped. I weighed pros and cons on that drive. I could quit my job, but I'd have to leave our church. The Eastern time zone has longer summer nights, but I'd have to say good-bye to my house. And on it went. Some of these I said aloud, but the blue sky!—oh, that Michigan sky spoke louder. All those Great Lakes must make the sunshine dazzle more in the Mitten State: the azure romanticized the weedy parking lots that welcomed us; the sky faded to periwinkle as we dined alone downtown, the streets all but deserted in the state capital on a weekend night in late summer.

"Could we really move here?" Dave asked.

I sipped my wine, staring out at the empty sidewalk. We'd walked by a bail bonds shop, vacant storefronts, and the domed capitol building. We snapped a selfie and smiled. Maybe, our expressions said. Maybe this could be home.

"Maybe." I sipped more wine.

This trip, the official second interview, was more a double date than interrogation. Dave's future boss took us on a tour of the city, the newspaper building, and even a local farmers' market. More questions came up about Lansing itself than about the actual job. What were the schools like? What about affordable housing? Each answer came as inevitability: Home? This? As we drove away from the city toward Wisconsin, I took in the boarded-up showrooms on overgrown car lots. The homes that had taken the recession hard. The liquor stores and pot shops with grates over windows. The congested suburban thoroughfares and the stoplights that turned red despite the lack of pedestrians or cars in the heart of downtown.

And the blue sky shone overhead, turned that stunning periwinkle at dusk.

The job offer came shortly thereafter, once we'd returned home. Dave laughed into the phone as he called me with the news. "So," he said, "want to move to Michigan?" I stood in the parking lot of Alice's pre-K, waiting to pick her up. "Um, wow. Wow. Dave," was all I could say. My church, I thought. My heart.

"God goes with you," my friend Amy said one night on my couch. "You're not going alone. You're being sent, Erin. I don't want you to go, but you're being sent."

So we went.

The first voices we encountered in this new wilderness were those in books; we had no friends here, no church yet, so books kept us company for many long months. We read David Platt, Francis Chan—and I'd set them on my bedside table and think, "Yes, but . . . we have fifty grand in debt." Then came Shane Claiborne's *The Irresistible Revolution*. His was a voice that resonated. We felt that the new monastics understood how we wanted to spend this life: diligently following Jesus; intentionally generous with our stuff, money, and time; and committed to a place. New monasticism is compelling to people who have just left their church home for a new state. It calls you to ground yourself, to stay put.

But as Dave and I read more, we realized we were reading these books in a vacuum. We needed a church community to help us discern how any of the marks could be translated into our context. Could we practice any of these marks in our rural rental without diluting them to the point of being inauthentic at best, harmful at worst? Could we, how could we—? We had so many questions, especially about where to even begin, with three kids and a load of debt.

Even as the questions continued over our first year in Lansing, our GPS brought us to a spot on the map where God was busy: Sycamore Creek Church. It was with gratitude that I stood stunned in the rhubarb patch that day when Sarah asked us to join the Arthurs' experiment in small things. They, and Sycamore Creek Church, didn't need us. We needed them.

We needed them not for socializing, though there's wisdom for homeschooling parents in leaving the living room once in a while, especially around February. We needed this covenantal friendship and the shared dinner once a week because nowhere else were our questions considered a healthy part of our formative growth rather than a nosy intrusion. These weekly dinners weren't about gathering fellow Shane Claiborne readers and geeking out about his most prophetic quotes. It wasn't a fan club; it was spiritual formation. It was, if you will, a baby step toward an *order*.

Like novitiates, if you're praying that God will speak through this new community, things get real, fast. Brace yourself for truth telling.

See, partway into our year of small things I was unhappy; something in our family life wasn't working. I live with depression, sure, but this was more than clinical. It was something I couldn't put my finger on. My soul was being crushed by something wearing an invisibility cloak. As I prepped a homeschooling lesson one December afternoon, I noticed a yellow school bus drive by our house. The next morning at breakfast, again. That afternoon, as I finished the lessons and was folding laundry, again. Again and again, I'd look up just at the right time. And I'd be longing for that bus to stop.

We had begun to homeschool because a teaching method that a friend was using back in Wisconsin resonated with us, the burned-out employees who saw their children for an hour or two a day. This bibliophile who worked more than full-time envisioned rest and renewal in days spent reading good books and exploring nature. But in practice, now that we were in Lansing, *snow*. So much snow. Our first two winters in Michigan were the worst on record for any human life anywhere (almost). And in practice, isolation: we were miles from everything. And in practice, my kids weren't learning with anyone but their burned-out mother. And in practice, we're a really white bunch in our house. The world doesn't look like us; it's much, much bigger.

What started as slow mornings reading and long afternoons outside became petty arguments between siblings, a strain in my voice. And meanwhile, I was reading all that Jesus, all that Shane Claiborne, all that Dorothy Day, all telling me to get out and serve my world; it was a recipe for incongruity. So partway through this year of small things, Tom spoke as a prophet (but don't tell him that).

"It sounds like homeschooling is the problem." French toast casserole and bacon took the edge off his statement at the parsonage dinner table that Tuesday.

"Homeschooling isn't really the problem," I argued. The girls and I were reading such good books!

"Or maybe it's where you live? You're really isolated out there." But, you know, we were in a lease. "You're stressed, and something's not working." Tom is never afraid to go on, and his voice remained calm and kind. "How do you see homeschooling and new monasticism working together? What about where you live?"

"I don't know. Yeah, I don't know."

When pieces of your life start to move because of this friendship, consider God to be at work. Be humble; be patient. Tears pooled in my field of vision. A toddler squirmed on my lap. I ate more bacon. Sarah nudged Tom along with a cough (he didn't catch her cue); she started picking up the dishes.

"We'll be praying for you," she said later as we put on gloves and coats. I knew they would. We hugged at the door. "We love you, friends."

We stewed and prayed about this together for months. Finally, while the Arthurs were visiting family in Florida in February (some people have all the luck), Dave and I decided that, at the semester's end, we would quit homeschooling. We sent an email, which Sarah says she raced outside to the pool (again, in February, but I'm not bitter) to share with Tom.

"I didn't think you'd actually do it," Tom laughed a week later, around the Tuesday dinner table again. We admitted we had no idea what came next.

"Yeah, so we're blaming you guys if this is a horrible mistake," I joked, putting forks and spoons on napkins, there at the table that had originally sparked this dramatic change. "Not really," I added.

"But kind of," Dave interjected. And the relief—oh, the relief—
that if disaster or winter struck again, the Arthurs would be there
with us too. Oh, the relief of that spiritual support.[2] This is a gift:
discernment in community can be a beautiful part of a life of listening. No longer can we be deaf to God's voice—not when we sense
our prayers and our friends' prayers pointing in the same direction.

Back to Sarah

This could be the hardest thing you do all year: not just finding
people who are willing to make vows to you in covenantal friendship, but listening, discerning, asking and being willing to hear
the tough questions. As Jon Stock says in *Inhabiting the Church:
Biblical Wisdom for a New Monasticism*,

> We might even call the practice of vow making prophetic, in that
> vow making will often prove to tell the truth to the world around
> us, and in that vow making will never fail to tell the truth to us
> who enter into vows. Our vows will always expose us to both the
> tragedies and joys that are the bane and the blessing of our hu-
> manity. Communities who live by vows may not always function
> as cities set on a hill, but, if they will be honest with themselves,
> they will always be confronted with the truth of who they are.[3]

Here's another snapshot of what we mean: One night back in
graduate school, those of us from Isaiah House found ourselves
at a potluck with another group of young adults who shared a
household. They were a bunch of grad students and activists and
urban gardeners who were trying the hippie/hipster thing but were
otherwise irreligious. When they heard us describe ourselves as
an intentional Christian community, one of them asked, "What
does that mean? What do you do that we don't do?"

We thought for a moment, then one of us replied, "Well, we
confess our sins to one another."

Awkward pause.

"Yeah," one of them finally said, "we don't do that."

You may have an ideal community in mind: the perfect housemates, the perfect hippie/hipster commune, the perfect network of
like-minded families. But you can't manufacture honest covenantal
community without the One who is the source of it: God in three
persons, Father, Son, and Holy Spirit. From before the beginning
of time, sharing holy, creative, joy-filled, beautiful, truth-speaking,
righteous, loving, selfless, empowering, healing, reconciling life.
From the Father to the Son, from the Son to the Father, through the
Holy Spirit, pouring into one another. Life that the Trinity offers to
the "other," the stranger, to those who are not God. Meaning: us.

Shared life within a truth-telling, covenantal friendship does
not begin with humans. You can't force it to happen, build it from
scratch with your grubby bare hands. It's not a matter of simply
finding a bunch of hipsters with cool glasses who are willing to
do unconventional things like share a car and grow kale in the
front yard (watch Erin back away slowly). You can't pull true community together through a book or a movement or even a year of
small things. It begins and ends with God, who is the One who
heals you and allows you to see others the way God sees them.
To paraphrase theologian Dietrich Bonhoeffer in his timeless *Life
Together*, if you're seeking community for the sake of community,
you will simply find disappointment.[4] If you're humbly seeking
to do God's will with others who are on a similar journey, you
will find authentic community thrown in—even with people you
never expected.

Awesome. So this year of small things begins with an impossible
task: build a human community that can't be built by humans.
Got it.

Oh, wait. That's what we call the church. Start there.

Our assumption is that you're already part of a worshiping
community, a local feet-on-the-ground group of Christ-followers
in your area. We've mentioned Acts 2:41–47. Read it tonight, then

again tomorrow, then every day for a couple of weeks. Pray. Email
it to a couple of friends you trust. Ask, "Am I reading this correctly,
or does our life look nothing like this?" Ask, "But could it? Just
an eensie bit?" Ask, "Why not?"

So start with your church. Maybe it doesn't look anything like
this. Hints and glimpses, perhaps, but not quite the rich vision that
we see in Acts 2. But chances are, there is one other person or family
in your church that is already doing something different: an older
couple that takes in foster kids; a youngish family that is aggres-
sively paying off debt so they can give more; a young woman who
volunteers at the homeless shelter once a month. Note that these may
not be people for whom you have a natural affinity. They may not
like the same food, listen to the same music, wear the same styles.
They may have never heard of any of the authors or activists we've
mentioned. Never mind. Consider sharing a meal with them, one
family or person at a time, and asking two simple questions: Why
do you choose to live differently? How can we be in this together?

Probe a bit. You're not merely asking how you can do the ministry stuff or the outreach stuff together. This is not about program
logistics. This is about sharing life. The daily stuff: meals, chores,
transportation—even, if it makes sense in your context, housing.
Tell them that you have been reading Acts 2 and are drawn to
the vision, asking yourself what the church, the world, your life
would look like if you lived this way. If you sense an openness to
continued conversation, plan another meal in which you share
about the year of small things. Perhaps begin reading this book
together. Map out a covenant. Set a start date. Begin.

By the end of one year, you will not necessarily have Acts 2.
It's certainly not what we have. Yours may be a small group, for
instance. Or a network of households. Or a virtual cohort whose
goal is to build little pockets of local communities over time. Or
just one other person, couple, or family that's at least willing to
have one more meal with you to talk about all this.

Small things. Remember?

~~~~~ *Questions for Reflection and Discussion* ~~~~~~~~

1. Who are your closest Christian friends? What draws you together?

2. How would they react if you asked them to hold you accountable to some of the more radical practices of downward mobility (paying off debt so you can give more, for instance)?

3. Who in your church is living in unusual, even radical, ways—even if it's in just one obvious area of life? How might you get to know these people better?

4. What might "shared life" look like in your context, within your faith community?

5. What is your greatest fear about entering into covenantal friendship?

~~~~~ *For Further Reading* ~~~~~~~~~~~~~~~~~~~~

Bonhoeffer, Dietrich. *Life Together*. San Francisco: HarperSanFrancisco, 1954.

Heath, Elaine A., and Larry Duggins. *Missional, Monastic, Mainline: A Guide to Starting Missional Micro-Communities in Historically Mainline Denominations*. Eugene, OR: Cascade Books, 2014.

Heath, Elaine A., and Scott T. Kisker. *Longing for Spring: A New Vision for Wesleyan Community*. Eugene, OR: Cascade Books, 2010.

Stock, Jon, Tim Otto, and Jonathan Wilson-Hartgrove. *Inhabiting the Church: Biblical Wisdom for a New Monasticism*. Eugene, OR: Cascade Books, 2007.

2

hospitality
beyond martha stewart

In the greeting let all humility be shown to the guests,
whether coming or going; with the head bowed down
or the whole body prostrate on the ground, let Christ
be adored in them as He is also received.

—The Rule of Saint Benedict (6th c.)

Sarah's Story

On our kitchen table sits a wooden prayer cube with a different
prayer on each side. When it comes time to pray before a meal,
sometimes we'll intentionally choose a side (for example, the
classic "Bless us, O Lord . . ."). Or we'll pick up the cube, roll
it around in our hands, and randomly settle on something. I
wouldn't say the prayers are particularly earth-shattering or that
they always speak for us or to us. But on one particular Sunday

four years ago, while our baby gurgled away over his applesauce
and Tom and I snatched a meal between the craziness of church
and evening meetings, the words of one prayer nearly knocked
us over.

We had just been lamenting how tired we were. Tom's pastoral
position was insanely demanding. I was still trying to freelance.
The baby had rocked our world forever. It just didn't seem possible to add hospitality to the mix, inviting someone to stay with
us who otherwise had nowhere to live. The basement wasn't even
finished, so without a guest room, where would the person sleep?
Plus, it was a parsonage, so we would likely have to do a bunch of
explaining to our church family. And yet we had both discerned—
separately—that perhaps it was time. We had gone too long without sharing our home with someone in need. "Hospitality to the
stranger" was a key mark of new monasticism, but what were we
doing about it? Meanwhile, here was a woman from our church
who was trying to get out of a tricky situation, trying to get back
on her feet, who seemed like a good fit.

But we knew what hospitality demands. We had done this thing
from the inside, in multiple different settings, both as a couple
and with community. Hospitality to the stranger, to the struggling, demands more than just a meal or a ride now and then. It
requires more than just a bed with clean sheets (although there are
multiple forms of hospitality, not just offering a room, which we'll
discuss shortly) or an extra set of towels in the bathroom—even
more than time, or money, or shared resources, or intentional
communication, or relinquishing your personal space. It demands
a complete overhaul of whoever you thought you were, whatever
you thought your life was about.

And meanwhile, like I said, the baby had already done that. In fact,
having a child after fourteen years of marriage was the single most
demanding act of hospitality we had ever tackled—and we'd taken
in strangers from homeless shelters, single teen moms with infants
and toddlers, "former" drug addicts, self-appointed prophetesses,

pathological liars, borderline paranoiacs, someone who looked *exactly* like the Unabomber, and the certifiably mentally ill.

So we were already tired. Did I mention how tired we were?

Tom picked up the prayer cube and read whatever was in front of him.

"O Lord Jesus, bless our home and bless our meal. Give us strength to share everything with those who are in hunger and need. Amen."

Silence.

"Well," he finally said after a moment. "There's our answer."

•••••

So there it is, right near the beginning of this year of small things: hospitality.

Last month the task was to create a covenantal friendship, to find others willing to take this journey with you. Now the very next step before you've even got the first one down—is to take that little vision of community and make it wider. Make it big enough to fit someone who, on a normal day, makes you uncomfortable. Make room for the other, the stranger, the one who does not look/ smell/act/talk/dress like you and who doesn't want to. Someone on the fringe, someone falling through the cracks, someone the rest of society warns you about.

Sharing life with those outside your socioeconomic enclave— that's radical hospitality in a nutshell. Welcoming Christ in the stranger—that's radical *Christian* hospitality in a nutshell. And it takes many forms. For us, it has meant opening up whatever spare space we have and making room for a short- or long-term housemate. For others, it means sharing a weekly meal around a table—not serving from above, giving handouts, but sitting like family together, breaking and passing bread. For others, it means offering the use of the washer and dryer, or sharing rides, or watching children, or taking meals to a shut-in, or any number of small-but-big things.

Hospitality is a key mark of new monasticism because it's a key mark of the gospel. God in Christ reached out to us, the other—gave up status, influence, power—to welcome strangers into shared life. As the apostle Paul says in Philippians 2:1–11 (ESV), Jesus "emptied himself," was willing to take whatever was his and pour it out, share it freely, suffer for those who are not God. Paul says nothing about whether we were "deserving," much less grateful. We were strangers, and our God not only welcomed us but became like a slave for our sake. Some of us cared, some of us responded, but most of us didn't. Yet he did it anyway.

So hospitality is the posture of Christ toward the world, and thus it is the posture of the Christian. But please note: this is not about being naturally gifted or even particularly good at whatever you think hospitality is. It's not about having some kind of Martha Stewart instinct for the select guest list, the well-laid-out table, hand-lettered place cards. It's about drawing on a power, on a love, that is beyond yourself entirely. "Give us strength," said the prayer on the cube. Not "give us the spiritual gift of hospitality." Not "make us naturally hospitable." Not even "give us margin in our schedules, free us from other commitments, line up all these other things so that we're clearly ready to practice hospitality."

Nope, just "give us strength."

And not merely "to share," but "to share *everything*."

Darn that cube. Or rather, bless that cube. Shortly afterward, we invited Tabitha over for a meal to tell her that our home was her home, if that's what she needed. We would be her family while she got back on her feet. All we could offer was a framed-out basement with a bare egress window, a concrete floor, an old queen-sized mattress, and some random furniture, but we could make it work if she was willing.

She was willing—nay, overjoyed—and thus a new member of our family moved in. We set her up as cozily as possible in the basement for a few months, then brought her bedroom up into my tiny office when the trustees began finishing the basement. As she built her cleaning business, attempted to find reliable transportation, and experienced setback after setback, we walked through those together. We had meals at least once a week, offered rides, checked in on a regular basis. She offered to babysit Micah faithfully every Friday while Tom and I went on a date—a gift she still gives us every week, to this day, because she's Tabitha.

And meanwhile she was there when Micah first scooted on his chubby knees across the living room. She was there when he took his first steps, said his first words, transitioned from diapers to the potty. She was there when I went into labor with Sam, helping Micah understand why Mommy kept wandering away to bellow unintelligible noises, hanging out with him while Tom rushed me to the hospital, loving that confused little boy till my parents arrived. This was no hotel, guests passing one another with a polite nod. This was sharing life.

Eventually Tabitha was able to get her own place. Our finished basement echoes with emptiness. So this year of small things, for the Arthurs, begins with a guest room downstairs and the question of what to do about it. It's a question that goes back fourteen years, nearly to the start of our marriage.

●●●●●

Snapshot, fourteen years ago: Let's just say that scrubbing long hair out of a toilet was not really my thing. Especially the hair of a male guest living in my house. Why *must* men make such a mess of toilets? It was an outrage. I was insulted. I was totally grossed out. I did not sign up for this.

Looking back, I'm not sure what I thought I had signed up for. Tom and I were living in our very first house, a quaint, moldering (and thus affordable), turn-of-the-century place that we had discovered on a back street in Petoskey, Michigan. We had never heard of new monasticism (was it even invented yet?), never witnessed radical hospitality.[1] But even before we moved in, we sensed that God wanted us to share our space somehow, that it was not, in fact, *our* space. We weren't sure what that looked like (foster children? exchange students? a boarder?)—I'm not even sure we knew it was called "hospitality," nor what that word could possibly mean beyond the cover of *Midwest Living*. But we were open.

Shortly after we moved in, through a complex series of events, we invited an older man from the homeless shelter where Tom volunteered once a week to live with us. He was quiet, studious, working a steady job six days a week making minimum wage, and even attended the Lutheran church when he could. So this was not a freebie. He would pay a very reasonable room and board, joining us for dinner each night. We would share the common living areas, including the only bathroom. He would help with dishes, take out the trash, and shovel snow. And we would all respect the quiet nature of our mutual lifestyles, which (sans kids) was downright monastic. Those were the very few "rules."

There was never the goal that our housemate would eventually rise to middle-class autonomy and leave us. Why should there be? Housing prices in our resort town meant that anyone attempting to go it alone on minimum wage would live in substandard conditions. We ourselves appreciated the income, especially once I quit full-time ministry and began freelance writing.[2] There was no mental illness or other major obstacles. Like Tabitha years later, he simply became part of the household.

If I make hospitality sound like a simple process, an idyllic arrangement that benefits everyone, please know that my heart— your heart, any human heart—is the biggest obstacle to this being so. Every guest, even one coming just for dinner, brings her or his own kind of mess: emotional, psychological, spiritual, and— most obviously—physical. Your space, your furniture, your clothing, none of it will look or smell the same. But guess what? You bring your own mess too. And on that toilet-scrubbing day several months after our guest joined us, my mess was the deeply ingrained sense that the whole arrangement was manifestly unfair. The addition of a stranger to our house was no longer frightening (we had been warned by many concerned people that we were living dangerously); it had descended to embittering. It made more work for me. I was just so tired.

Make it a gender thing. Make it a class thing. If he had been some other ethnicity, I no doubt would have made it a race thing, God help me. But it was wrong. And partway through the scrubbing, as I wiped out a wad of long hair with a filthy piece of paper towel, it struck me: Jesus, while he lived on earth, maybe had long hair.

"I was a stranger, and you welcomed me" (Matt. 25:35 ESV). I knew nothing of new monastic hospitality, but I knew my Bible. And there it was. I had welcomed a poor, homeless stranger into my house, which meant that Jesus had walked through the door, just as he had walked through Martha and Mary's door in Luke 10:38–42. He had plopped his stuff down in the guest room, eaten the food, his totally human body doing totally human things, like shedding long Galilean hair. I'm pretty sure he was not particularly obsessive about ancient Near Eastern hygiene; we are given no stories of him carefully picking crumbs off the table after the Last Supper, for instance. So wherever he went, someone cleaned up after him. And if their hearts were right, they said, "When else do you get to clean up after the living God? It is my honor. Pick me."

Pick me.

•••••

Hospitality to the stranger is not just a one-time event. It's a cycle that repeats itself as you grow and falter, grow and falter in the journey of becoming more like Jesus. It doesn't matter if you're inviting refugees to dinner, offering your washer and dryer to a single mom on public assistance, or tithing a room. At some point you will arrive at a crisis. You will land somewhere on a spectrum of annoyed, frustrated, angry, bitter, even betrayed. And from there you either become broken and aware of Christ in your midst—which is the opportunity to become open again—or you shut down.

One of the ways to weather the crisis is to practice hospitality in community. Because one of the many, many things Isaiah House taught me is that whatever I think is "my" space or "my" time or "my" stuff is an illusion—and that the crisis in hospitality always comes with that word "my." As soon as you enter into community with others, you begin to realize that it requires opening your fists. You begin to release your space. You begin to alter your schedule. You begin to share your stuff. Because none of it is actually yours. And when the community takes that basic principle and begins purposefully applying it to strangers, to the poor and disenfranchised, you have both support and accountability. Yes, you're nuts. But a handful of other people are nuts too.

During those three years living in Isaiah House, Tom and I learned very quickly that the kind of hospitality we were offering—to women and children in transition—was nearly impossible for us as individuals or even as couples. At one point the only person in our household of twelve who had a full-time job was Rebecca, a physical therapist—and still she took on more than her share of cooking dinner and working the garden and managing children. Any one of us members, when left alone with all the guests for the weekend, found the weight of the household tipping toward instability like a ship without ballast. There were too many personalities to navigate, too many chores and responsibilities to negotiate, too many histories of dysfunction—including our own—all colliding under one roof. As soon as the rest of the members returned, the ship seemed to right itself. Practicing hospitality in that context required a community of people willing to share the burdens and risks of such an adventure.

Both Christine Pohl in her book *Making Room* and Elizabeth Newman in *Untamed Hospitality* give the historical and theological context for how hospitality was central to the early Christian communities, in direct contrast to the stratified social orders of the ancient world. Indeed, for the old monastic orders, including the Benedictines, making room for fellow believers of all backgrounds as well as for strangers was a nonissue: it was simply what Christians did. And yet this practice has gotten lost over time, particularly for white, upwardly mobile Americans, in part because shared life in general has eroded. We inhabit single-family units, which means, if hospitality is to be practiced, there's just one person or family bearing the burdens and risks of opening one's life to a stranger. It sounds overwhelming, even terrifying, so we don't do it at all.

When Tom and I first left Isaiah House for our suburban parsonage, it would've been easy to hunker down into single-family-dom. But our new church became our teacher in this area, helping us enlarge our imaginations for the many forms that hospitality can take: everything from giving rides to church for women from the homeless shelter to offering your couch to a friend in trouble—not to mention the countless ways our congregation opened up its homes and lives to us, total strangers, making us feel instantly welcome. So we didn't have to go it alone—in fact, in chapter 8 we'll share about the meal we organized with other folks in our congregation who were practicing somewhat radical forms of hospitality, just so those folks could look around the table and say, "Hey, I'm not crazy! I can learn from these people. I'm not alone."[3]

For the Wasingers, like many at Sycamore Creek, it's often through the local church that God first calls us to welcome strangers. It's in community that we find the grace and support we need to even give it a try.

Erin's Story

Our adventures in Christian hospitality began several years ago, back in Wisconsin. Days after Louisa was born, Dave and some friends from Water City Church held signs and warmly greeted a family of refugees as they walked into the terminal of a tiny airport on a February night. Nangshwe, her husband Wai Hin, and their preschooler piled into our van to drive to the small apartment that they would call home. That's how it started.

Or maybe our foray into holy, simple hospitality began in the weeks before that, as Dave and I spread out groceries on our own dining-room table, my third baby kicking my ribs as we tallied bread, milk, and apples to stock their empty refrigerator. (And bricks of cheese: "What is this?" Wai Hin asked us Wisconsinites a few weeks later.)

Or maybe hospitality began even before that, as Amy and I coordinated donations from our church of things like dressers, toys, dishes, a kitchen table, and a couch. (And a toaster, which we later explained to our new friends was best used *before* spreading butter on bread: "Oh yes, that explains the smoke.")

Or maybe, actually, it began even earlier around a café table when I met with a friend from church who at the time was director of Oshkosh's newly reopened World Relief office. He'd invited a group of his acquaintances from around the city to pitch us a crazy idea: What if area churches formed teams to welcome the refugee families that the office would be working with in the coming months? Dave and I had been invited to the meal because we were journalists after a good story. We left with our hearts pounding and our blood pulsing.

"This. We need to do this," Dave said as we walked from the café, past our church, and back to the newspaper office where we both worked. That was it: I passed the story to one of my best reporters and dove head-first, heart-first, into hospitality, our church beside us. The time we spent with the family was shared life. We gave them rides to school and work. We lingered over coffee at their kitchen table. We occasionally babysat their daughter during Nangshwe's language class and even drove them to the ER when their toddler was ill, helping translate the doctor's instructions to the terrified parents. We celebrated a birthday and when Wai

Hin landed a wonderful job. This May, we celebrated from afar as they purchased their first home.

By comparison, the hospitality Dave and I have offered in this year of small things is, well, small. So small. Other than giving rides to folks from church, babysitting so a single mom could go to class, or making meals for a homeless ministry, Dave and I have struggled to wrestle this hospitality beast to the ground in a way that rocked our boat quite like Nangshwe and Wai Hin had. Some of it was our newness to the Lansing area; some, our social isolation in our rural rental. Some of it, to be frank, was my own struggle with depression, which makes even small things feel impossible. So in the end, despite feeling like hospitality flunkies, our small moment this year wasn't even of our own manhandling; it was pure grace.

Here's where the months of thinking and praying and talking about hospitality finally led us: One Saturday in March I made sweet potato fries (fist pump for saving the world!). Dave and I showed up at Tom and Sarah's, the kids at Grandma's for the weekend and the Pyrex full of starch in my hands like a small offering. Sarah was bustling around her kitchen, too overwhelmed with new recipes to articulate how we might be able to assist her. Dave and I made small talk with another couple from church, Paul and Marian, about our excitement to see the local theater company perform that night.

This is hospitality so simple: Sarah beckoned us over to our chairs. Tom poured us water or wine. I blessed the meal with the Arthurs' prayer cube, and we sat together. That's it.

Wait. You've got to know Paul and Marian.

Marian's voice singing into the microphone at Sycamore Creek Church preceded any formal introductions when we first started attending there. She's not a stereotypical church musician: she's got a mohawk, a "whoop, whoop!" that bursts out during sermons like an "amen," a fiery sense of justice, and no filter to stop her from calling it like it is. She's a musical prodigy: she can play anything on the keyboard—*anything*. She's also blind. Her husband, Paul, volunteers at church too, mowing lawns and serving on the media team. They live in the trailer park across the road from Tom and Sarah.

This dinner would not be happening without Jesus, I thought, glancing around the table at the six of us. Nowhere in our lives do our biographies intersect—until Jesus. And in Jesus, we found family.

By the grace of sweet potatoes and the Spirit, and some theater tickets gifted to Tom, we found ourselves laughing and getting to know one another. And that's the thread that runs throughout this small act of hospitality: knowing each other.

We drew our circle of community, and then we made it wider. And we hope to do the triple date again soon. A small thing, but a big step in grace.

Back to Sarah

Unlike publicly recognized communities of hospitality like Rutba House or the Simple Way or even Isaiah House, few of us are likely to have strangers knocking on our doors. So this month begins with simply looking around. Someone in your orbit is not like you, someone whose circumstances challenge everything you thought you believed about middle-class comfort. Where do you begin?

As with building covenantal friendship last month, start with your church. It's no secret that the New Testament urges believers to reach out to the poor. But the biblical writers assume that *these are people you know*: fellow Christians who worship with you, break bread with you, pray with you. In the early church, the poor were not some class unto themselves to which the church had to reach out; they were deeply embedded in the body, so that their suffering was everyone's suffering.[4]

Let me state this boldly: if there are no poor people in your church, something isn't right. Somewhere the gospel of reconciliation—between God and people, between races and classes and cultural distinctions—has gone awry. Without the poor in your church, there is no opportunity for real friendship, for fellowship across socioeconomic lines, which, as I've said, is one of the best visions the New Testament gives us for the kind of friendship God offers humanity.

Odds are, however, there are at least *some* people in your church who are struggling—especially given the massive economic changes in our country over the past decade. And if they aren't in your church, they're related to people in your church, or they clean your church. As a longtime missionary once said, if you're not sure what God is calling you to do, do what's in front of you. Say hello to that stranger you've somehow never noticed. Get to know her by name. Bring her a cup of coffee. Take her out to lunch. Invite her family over for dinner. Then for Thanksgiving. Let her reciprocate. At the same time, don't expect a thank-you. (Do your friends thank you when you text them, like you're some kind of hero for wanting to be their friend?) This is about building friendship, not setting up structures in which you get to practice benevolence. See where the adventure takes you. Pray. All the time. Jesus just might show up at your door.

•••••

Fast-forward again. I'm sitting at my desk sipping a cup of coffee that Tabitha made for me. A few months into our year of small things, Tom and I have discerned that she needed a break again from the fray, a chance to regroup. So she's moved back in. It's a battle for her, this feeling that she's taken a step backward. Things have not gone as planned. But she is miles ahead of where she was when she joined us the first time, four years ago. And meanwhile she *is* our family, seamlessly moving back into the rhythms of our life together, making extra coffee for me—just because, out of love—before she dashes off to work.

Christ, no longer a stranger, handing me a cup of coffee that I don't deserve.

Jesus in the small things.

~~~~~ *Questions for Reflection and Discussion* ~~~~~~~~

1. What aspects of radical hospitality do you find compelling? What about it perhaps strikes a chord of fear?
2. What might hospitality look like in your context, given your current circumstances?
3. In what ways might your covenant community and/or your church provide opportunities and support for practicing radical hospitality?
4. If you were to take one baby step in practicing hospitality this month, what would it be?

~~~~~ *For Further Reading* ~~~~~~~~~~~~~~~~~

Newman, Elizabeth. *Untamed Hospitality: Welcoming God and Other Strangers*. Grand Rapids: Brazos, 2007.

Pohl, Christine D. *Making Room: Recovering Hospitality as a Christian Tradition*. Grand Rapids: Eerdmans, 1999.

Wilson-Hartgrove, Jonathan. *Strangers at My Door: A True Story of Finding Jesus in Unexpected Guests*. New York: Convergent Books, 2013.

3

radical finances

> It's not God's standard operating procedure to rain
> bread from heaven. . . . Instead, God invites us into the
> abundance of eternal life through economic relation-
> ships with other people.
>
> —Jonathan Wilson-Hartgrove[1]

Erin's Story

Sarah was stirring stroganoff at my stove (the same night we realized she was almost fatally allergic to our dog). Daylight saving
time had just begun; against the backdrop of the dark evening
outside, the patio door reflected an image of Tom hovering over
Dave's laptop at the kitchen island. Kid drama erupted sporadi-
cally from the living room. We adults did our best to ignore it,
while peeking in to ensure that Sam hadn't eaten any marbles.

"Okay, what am I looking at?" Tom expanded pie charts and financial categories on the budget Dave had created online.

Meanwhile, Tom's color-coded budget spreadsheet for the year was on another screen, anticipating just about every financial category you'd imagine. By contrast, Dave and I had forgotten to factor in the car insurance for three months. (Adulting is hard.)

"I want more details," Tom said, getting frustrated with our far-too-simple outline for living simply. We toggled to another view in order to go deeper, to sniff out how we had spent that twenty bucks at the hardware store.

Most polite company would keep the subject to preschool or maybe politics, at least until the broccoli was finished steaming. Not our style. Here we were, beginning October by sharing our budget with friends in covenantal community. "Well that's . . . interesting," my mom said when I told her about our dinner plans that night.

Small talk just isn't our thing.

•••••

The topic of money fell early in our yearlong experiment because it's rare for any of the other new monastic practices to not involve some dollars and cents. Sharing a meal or a spare bedroom will cost you something; going out of your way to pick up someone from church will too. Because these are practices we value, we have to be wise about how we can make them happen. But more importantly, early on we realized the vital nature of being radically vulnerable with your community about what you spend. Proceed with caution.

Meanwhile, as we raise young children, we're already thinking about what sort of messages we're passing along about living simply, shopping justly, and giving generously with kids who still love a big haul under the Christmas tree (more on that in chapter 5). Chances are they won't learn generosity simply by osmosis, so conversing about where our money goes keeps our families accountable and transparent at all ages, in social settings or at home. For instance, because the Arthurs started the allowance train, we were spurred to also. Our girls now have three jars— give, save, and spend—and they break their allowances into equal thirds.[2] On Sundays, they carry their "give" jars to Sycamore Creek Church's kids program to clank their dimes and quarters into a basket for missions. And we talk about this often, from how much money the cowboy hat that Alice pines for costs to why we give back to God and why we give to others in generous proportion.

Our weekly conversations around the table turn to money almost every time because nearly all twelve marks of new monasticism (relocation, hospitality, care for the earth, etc.) immediately present obstacles of debt and dollars. For instance, if we believe that to care for the earth means avoiding pesticides on our fruit and vegetables, how will we pay for the organic strawberries? If we're aiming to live debt-free, what do we do when the car and the stove fail us in the same week? What does "sharing economically with our community and the needy" look like when the seven-year-old is asking for a bigger allowance and the children's teeth are growing in crookedly? (Please: if you know of a radical Christian orthodontist, send us that info ASAP.) How do we relocate if student loans or a mortgage are sinking us?

And let's be real: How do we even talk about this with one another?

First, it's awkward. Second, those children. I mean really, we throw around the words "budget," "insurance," and "mortgage" even as we're pleading with our kids to eat their veggies while cutting up their hot dogs. (Wasinger girls, for the record, don't like organic hot dogs—as if we could afford them.) Any financial planner worth her salt would clear her throat after about ten minutes of this and say politely, "Why don't you call me back when you're . . . when they graduate?"

And how do you *do* all of this—not simply rise above the status quo but live in solidarity with those around you who struggle?

How do you do this humbly, without defending every dollar you spend or every penny you save?

We're trying to figure that out. We haven't landed this plane after a year of attempts, if that gives you peace of mind. But our church is giving us some clues.

•••••

In terms of economics, Sycamore Creek's seats are filled with people who are all over the map—those who arrive with their families from a well-kept Lansing suburb and those who ride over together from the women's shelter. The debt-free and the burdened, we're all there.

The prayer team knows that the poor will always be among us (see Mark 14:7) because reminders appear in the weekly prayer requests: for jobs, for provision, for housing. The names sometimes change, but people in our church continually struggle with homelessness, debt, unemployment, and poor health. Obviously, we don't want folks to always remain poor and needy, so we work on this in various ways. But meanwhile money's not a taboo topic at SCC. Tom will toss up the Arthurs' budget on a screen (where some balk at the grocery budget, while others wonder how they survive, and Sarah squirms uncomfortably). At least once a year, our teaching team preaches a series on money, giving, and tithing.

We aren't just coaching people on personal finances, though we do encourage smart money principles using a variety of resources. Tom casts a vision for generosity too. Consider the past couple of Christmas Eve services. The tradition at SCC is for the entire holiday offering to go to local and international missions. From 2008 to 2012, SCC (whose attendance on a regular weekend now averages around 220) received an average of $3,600 on Christmas Eve. But for the past two years, for the entire season of Advent, we have encouraged one another to give away as much as we spend on our Christmas budget (more on that in chapter 5). A tidal wave of giving followed. When Tom proposed the giving challenge in

2013 and repeated it the following season, the average giving over those two holidays was nearly triple the average giving from the previous five years: almost $10,000.

But the dollar amount isn't the point. Don't trip over it being more or less than any spectacular holiday service where you happen to worship. Instead, consider the culture that can ask and generate enthusiasm for radical giving. Consider the conversations over coffee about how to explain to small children, or to extended family, what it means to give away the same as (or more than) what you spend during the holidays.

Consider that this church truly does give away the entire Christmas Eve offering—and not just to some ethereal idea of "missions" but to real people, in real locations, whose names and communities we know. For more than a decade, we've supported a Nicaraguan medical doctor and her friends who run a food and worship program for kids from her home in Managua. Twice a year, our church member Teresa—a local labor and delivery nurse—and other volunteers hop a plane to Nicaragua for about a week to work with Dr. Mirtila Padilla, ministering to more than a hundred people a day through medicines and spiritual counseling and playing with the children.

This sort of generosity spills out because we prompt one another beyond the holidays. It's not just about giving because it feels good; it's about sharing life. Some stock others' refrigerators when the months are longer than the checks. Some folks give rides or clothes. Some, like the Arthurs, share openly about what they spend. Radical vulnerability, leaving no line item taboo.

So if Dave and I were going to embed ourselves in this community—but even more, join in covenantal friendship with these crazy Arthurs—we had to move our family budget from the decade-long, unicorns-and-dragons mental trip to the uncompromising squares of a computer spreadsheet. We had to start from scratch, again, because each baby threw us for a loop in our debt-repayment schedule. We had to admit we needed a lot

of help, and we had to learn to get over ourselves long enough
to share our messy-math budget with Sarah and Tom. (So many
rectangles! I cannot.)

Over the year, constantly checking the temperature of our budget led to grace and challenges, especially as we dovetailed our
conversations about money with those of new monasticism. We
Wasingers moved this year—bought a house, in fact (more on
that soon). We paid off a loan this year. We didn't apply for that
alluring, higher-paying job out East this year.

Without someone else looking on in encouragement, how do
you learn to be more generous? How do you begin to save without hoarding or do more than panic when thinking about those
future orthodontist appointments?[3] It's difficult to do these things
without planning and prayer, but in community we're challenged
to do both more often.

It's hard to be generous in December if you've not been planning for it in October.

Or the December a year out, Tom would clarify.

Tom and Sarah are so good at this. But even they found a challenge in our budget-sharing relationship.

Sarah's Story

On the Tuesday night that we shared our financial spreadsheets,
Erin and Dave were clearly nervous. They hovered around the
kitchen island, pulling out pots and colanders, setting the table,
laughing in awkward bursts at Tom's matter-of-fact questions.
Tom, meanwhile, is an old hat at financial vulnerability. As Erin
said, he's been known to put our family spreadsheet up on the
screen during the Sunday morning message. Nothing fazes him.

"Fifty dollars per month for internet," he read absently from
the Wasingers' budget, scrolling down the lines. "Six hundred
dollars for groceries . . ."

My spoon clattered into the stroganoff. "*What*?!"

I looked over Tom's shoulder at the screen. "That's it? For five of you and a dog—and Lou still in diapers?"

"Yeah," Erin said with a shrug, "it's a stretch. Plus we're making dinner once a month for the overnight shelter downtown, the one on Sycamore Street."

I shifted to our laptop and scanned that same line item on our budget, which wasn't so much a goal but Tom's best guess based on averages from the past six months or so: $850. For two grown-ups, a three-year-old, and a nursing infant wearing his brother's hand-me-down cloth diapers. And we weren't bringing monthly meals to a homeless shelter, nor even offering hospitality to anyone in our home—yet.

"Dude," I said, which was about as theologically profound as my budget suddenly looked. "We flunk at this."

Right in front of us stood our challenge for financial simplicity in the month of October, one line item on a complicated spreadsheet, one small but significant thing: groceries.[4]

Forgive me if I wax mostly nontheological in this section. This is really just the on-the-ground details of the Arthurs' relationship with food—the theological point being, if nothing else sinks in about this chapter, we hope that radical financial vulnerability is seared in your brain forever and ever, amen. The Wasingers know what we spend, which is another way of saying the church knows what we spend, which means they can ask us, anytime, if what we're doing lines up with the biblical vision of God's economy. And tally up all the New Testament's references to food (or, say, just the parables of Jesus alone), and it's clear we're in good company. Uncomfortable company, but good.

We've been sensitive to issues of sustainability when it comes to the food supply in this country—on this planet, for that matter. We'll go into more detail in chapter 10 when we discuss creation care, but the short version is: the Arthurs have thought a lot about this. For most of our married life, Tom has been our primary cook, so when we moved here six years ago and I took over cooking and grocery shopping, I'd wander aisles cluelessly. I went with what I thought I knew: buy local and organic, cook mostly vegetarian (as we had at Isaiah House), avoid stuff with GMOs or hormones or whatever, and when you see "high-fructose corn syrup" listed anywhere on anything, run. I had no sense of what was reasonable to pay for food or even what was necessary in our basic supply. I just bought.

Meanwhile, every couple of months Tom and I would say, "Why are finances so tight all the time? Something's not working." The direct connection between what we were spending on, say, hormone-free organic milk and our actual income just didn't compute. *Duh.*

We knew that sustainability matters: where food comes from, who it benefits, who is hurt by our choices. However, sustainability and financial simplicity are not necessarily the same thing—at least not for the Arthurs. Not to mention that what may pass for "sustainability" might actually be a foodie form of conspicuous consumption. If we were going to live more simply when it came to finances—spending less so we could give more, so we could break the yokes of debt and consumerism—*maybe we would need to buy regular milk.*

A small thing, I know. Some of you can skip this section. But it was new for us.

And that wasn't all. It was also about all the food we already had, staring back at us from the crowded pantry and freezer. The half bag of frozen corn that wasn't enough for a full side dish. The six cans of white beans for the chili I never made because I suddenly learned, after all these years, that beans in general are not Tom's favorite. The leftover mashed sweet potatoes that I forgot were in the back of the freezer. If we were truly living in solidarity with the global poor, I began to realize, we'd eat this stuff, whether we like it or not, because *that's what we have.*

A few weeks after our dinner with the Wasingers, I pulled out a notepad and pencil. At the top I wrote "Meals from the Pantry and Freezer" and then took the notepad over to the fridge, opened the freezer door, and began making a list: frozen veggies for stir fry, pork chops that Tom found on sale, and on it went. Next I headed to the pantry and did the same. Bracket for a moment that my husband and children may not enjoy any of these things. That's what we had.

By the time I was done, there were twenty-one complete dinners on my list. *Twenty-one.* Almost enough for the entire month of November, especially if you factored in traveling for Thanksgiving. I'd have to purchase the usual perishable items, but otherwise dinners were set.

So that's what we did, we Arthurs, for the month following that financial "Come to Jesus" conversation. I bought almost nothing beyond basics and toiletries. Our pantry and freezer inventories shrank and shrank. My preschooler complained often and loudly. My husband shrugged; beans were still not his favorite. But our spending shrank too, and I was on a spiritual high for months.

I wish I could say it continued, that we had ongoing budgeting successes after that. But in time we realized that we had to stock the now-empty pantry with *something*. And slowly we slipped back into habits of spending too much. We stopped paying attention, stopped planning, became mortally tired of watching our preschooler's eyes fill with tears when we set his dinner plate in front of him. "What? I wanted hot dogs." Halfway through this year of small things, we were failing. Again.

And then, through an unlikely source, Tom had a budgeting breakthrough. During the winter he rather begrudgingly participated in Dave Ramsey's Financial Peace University, which was being held at our church—"begrudgingly" because Tom didn't need to add one more thing to his calendar, and because we already practiced a lot of what Ramsey talks about, especially regarding debt and tithing. We also have a few quibbles with FPU, including the basic principle that we're supposed to "live like no one else" now so that later we can "live (and give) like no one else." Really? It's all about getting to the point where you can pay cash for that swimming pool, with extra for charity? Or is it about living simply now so you can live simply later so the poor can simply live?

Tom joined the class anyway, in solidarity with the many people in our congregation who desperately needed it—and, lo, he learned something. After years of struggling to find the best program for budgeting, he picked up the simple idea of planning by paycheck, not by month. Yes, living from paycheck to paycheck, as they say. And meanwhile, he realized, we needed to practice by going to cash envelopes.

"So what's our budget for groceries?" he said on the day we started.

"Three hundred dollars per paycheck," I said firmly. Six hundred dollars per month.

Game on, Wasingers.

Finally—finally—after all those months, we hit our stride. On the days Tom gets paid, one of us heads to the bank and stuffs our various categories of envelopes with the designated amounts of cash, and I head to the store with $150 for that week's groceries. I'm learning very quickly what is worth spending money on: the store-brand version of basics, organic items and free-range meat only when they're on sale, *maybe* ice cream on the weeks I don't have to buy baby wipes or allergy medicine. I still avoid high-fructose corn syrup, shop at the farmers' market, and grow kale all summer (sorry, Erin). Coupons baffle me, but every once in a while I have a savings win—and earn points toward gas along the way.

Later, when we added Tabitha to the mix, I saw it as a fun challenge: we're now five, like the Wasingers.

We could do this.

Financial vulnerability for the win.

Back to Erin

Living simply and paying off debt is a bit like trudging up an icy driveway to some sketchy apartment complex late at night to deliver pizzas to someone who may or may not tip. In short, it's a drag.

Trust us: Dave spent the worst eight months of our lives delivering pizzas after working at the newspaper all day. During one of the coldest and snowiest winters in Michigan history. We pushed that Ramsey-inspired debt snowball around until Dave's frozen toes were numb and I was weepy every time we'd chuck another pile of tip money in our gaping hole of loans: student loans, a car loan, a loan to cover the cost of selling our home in Wisconsin at a big loss, and a hospital bill. Fifty thousand dollars made us crazy: first because we felt trapped, then because the strategy to repay that debt robbed us of energy to live, let alone raise three kids in a new place—during a winter that was sometimes colder than Alaska.

We took a desperate measure or two: tithed more, for one. Second, I took some advice from Shane Claiborne and used my retirement fund to pay off my student loan—despite overwhelming advice that I should only do that if I wanted to eat cat food in my old age.[5] I took a very part-time job at Sycamore Creek Church; Dave quit the pizza place.

And we quit being, as Ramsey would say, so "gazelle" about becoming debt-free that we couldn't find time to spend together, with the kids, serving our church, or out in our community.

We can't make debt-free living our goal. We can't make a cushy retirement account our goal. Those are good, responsible moves, and it's not sinful or bad to provide for yourself and your family. (We still aim to live debt-free, but . . . orthodontia, you know?) The problem lies in making the comfort of wealth our *goal.* Simplicity isn't even the goal, however you define it.

The goal is formation in the way of Christ, practiced and discussed in community, through meeting needs in relationships around us. When we become myopic about anything but this, we find our energy draining to an unrelenting power suck: "[Money] is a god demanding an all-inclusive allegiance."[6]

I'm reminded of the story of Joseph, after he interprets Pharaoh's dreams to mean there would be seven years of abundant crops followed by seven years of famine (Gen. 41). He instructs the Egyptians to store part of their bumper crops, and I think this is where some of us get caught. Don't our anxiety levels spike when the bank account dips? Don't we feel good with the bumper crop? But remember, this isn't the end of the story. It isn't about chucking money into the mattress just in case.

Rather than becoming the personal story of one man's rescue, Genesis 41 ends with God saving his *people*. The grain Joseph saved isn't just for his wife and sons or simply for his own brothers. Those piles in savings become the means of survival not for just one family but for *all* of God's people, the whole community. Pragmatically, this doesn't mean we should all give our grain to the government to hold for us until the rains stop and the earth parches. Rather, the story begs us to stop scrawling our own names on the doors of our silos and instead start seeing how our grain—our savings, our discretionary cash, the educations we've purchased—could help God's people, our communities, our churches.

This is uncomfortable stuff. You won't be the only one to wonder why someone didn't foresee the seven years of famine or why others couldn't work a little harder, at least as hard as you (Father, forgive us). You won't be the only one to groan that the need is so much or that it's so messy to mix relationships and money. But it's in the groaning and in the opening of the storehouses that we get closer to the character of Christ.

Our tension, then, in covenantal relationship is to constantly seek advice and grace about our money.

"Dave's pizza job is killing us," I told Sarah that winter, before our year of small things had even begun.

"Hmm," she said. And I know now, after the fact, that she was thinking, "Ditch the stupid snowball and save your marriage, save your sanity." But we weren't in covenantal friendship yet. We hadn't asked for this kind of input. And yet her "hmm" was a hint that she was someone with whom I could be vulnerable. It was almost like permission.

A few weeks later, Dave quit.

●●●●●

So let's bring it down to squares and rectangles. You want to practice some of the marks of new monasticism; you want to dive into a year of small things. But then, who's paying for these acts of hospitality to the stranger, the poor, the least of these? Because it's costly. It's not impossible or an unworthy pursuit, but if you're not giving until you notice it in your budget, perhaps you're not giving enough.

Or maybe you need to set a budget to begin with. It's hard to be flexible when you have no concept of where the money goes.

And meanwhile, debt. We know: it's real. It's not going away on its own, and rarely does it disappear easily. How will your community hold you accountable?

Have you asked your covenantal friends to push you toward more vulnerability and generosity? Have you set a time with them to workshop budgets, debt, and giving? (Bring food—it helps break the ice.) After a few sessions, notice how the conversation becomes less strained and emotionally charged. Making ourselves vulnerable with a select group of trusted people dismantles the power that money can have on our lives.

And instead of just making a plan to be more generous later—when the debt's paid, when the kids are done with college, when you retire, after you die—that vulnerability pushes you to create a roadmap for getting there sooner.

⁂

Right after our year of small things ended, I put a pot of water on the stove to boil. Spaghetti was on the menu: cheap, easy, bath-night ready. As I folded laundry in the corner, though, I noticed after the first, then second loads that no steam rose from beneath the lid.

"Dave, don't freak out, but the stove isn't working," I said, my hand hovering over the lukewarm burner.

He went into his quiet freak-out mode, pulling at burners and flipping switches and fuses.

"Will it ever stop?" He spoke through gritted teeth. The day before, the estimate for a car repair came in over the value of the car—the same vehicle for which we'd paid six hundred dollars to fix a different problem the month before. I'd spent more than our allotted cash at the grocery store three days prior. The doctor's office had called about a bill for a visit that insurance didn't cover.

We finished the spaghetti in the microwave (just . . . don't) and called the girls to eat, and I stewed about all those rectangles on our budget, all the sighs I heard from Dave. *Will it ever stop?*

This is a good place to pause. If we're honest, the stove thing was merely an annoyance. We could drain the savings or buy a new appliance with an installment plan. But if we viewed our dying stove as an opportunity for conversion, that moment was a gift. If we were bearing one another's burdens in community, we would remember this stress: it's the everyday, material reality of the poor with whom we share life.

And, too, we knew we weren't alone. We texted our covenantal friends to please, please pray for us. "Yes," Sarah said. "We'll pray. And we love you."

Tom texted back: "I'll bring over dinner Tuesday. All of it. Just relax."

Throughout this year of small things, we could hear echoes of Jesus's teachings from the mount: "Do not worry about tomorrow" (see Matt. 6:19–34 NIV). Jesus hinted that the kingdom of heaven is countercultural, grounded in relationships. In that context, perhaps the worst thing we could do would be to simply wait for God to step in with material blessings. Instead, as the Arthurs showed us, what if we worry not about our *own* tomorrow but about one another's tomorrow? What if we concern ourselves with making sure one another's bodies, one another's lives—including the poor in our midst—are whole and healthy? Then the small turn of expectations—like the year of small things—has big implications.

So yes, we worried about our stove. But we laughed a little instead of sulking as we went to bed. We felt supported, prayed for. "We'll figure it out," Dave said in a hopeful voice. Hope where hours before there had been none? Must be God at work in our community, in our small prayers, in these small but radical practices.

~~~~~ *Questions for Reflection and Discussion* ~~~~~

1. On a scale of 1 to 10 (1 being petrified, 10 being totally okay), how comfortable are you sharing your budget with others in covenant friendship?
2. Where do you struggle most with regard to finances?
3. What are your financial goals for the next year? The next five? How would you like to be remembered for using your money?
4. If you have children, what steps do you take to teach them about money and giving? Or, at the other end of the spectrum, as your parents age, how are you engaging them in conversations about long-term care, insurance, and other end-of-life financial decisions?
5. How does your church economically support its members and the needy in your city? What more could you do to share financial life?

~~~~~ *For Further Reading* ~~~~~

Campolo, Tony, and Shane Claiborne. *Red Letter Christians: What If Jesus Really Meant What He Said?* Nashville: Thomas Nelson, 2012.

Foster, Richard J. *Money, Sex and Power: The Challenge of the Disciplined Life*. New York: HarperCollins, 1985.

Johnson, Kelly S. *The Fear of Beggars: Stewardship and Poverty in Christian Ethics*. Grand Rapids: Eerdmans, 2007.

Sider, Ronald J. *Rich Christians in an Age of Hunger: Moving from Affluence to Generosity.* 5th ed. Nashville: Thomas Nelson, 2005.

————. *The Scandal of the Evangelical Conscience: Why Are Christians Living Just Like the Rest of the World?* Grand Rapids: Baker Books, 2005.

Wilson-Hartgrove, Jonathan. *God's Economy: Redefining the Health and Wealth Gospel.* Grand Rapids: Zondervan, 2009.

4

reclaiming spiritual habits

If the spiritual life doesn't lead us to freedom and grace,
then we've probably missed the point.

—Nathan Foster[1]

Erin's Story

I'm always game for trying new spiritual practices, but only the smallest practices last. For example, at one point I attempted to institute noon prayer with my children. Sure, we already prayed before meals—at lunch we sing "Thank You, Jesus" to the tune of "Frère Jacques"—but after reading Bonhoeffer's *Life Together*, I had grand visions of taking a couple of minutes to reflect on the goodness of God at the top of our day. Bonhoeffer suggests families use a devotion and a song, which sounded completely doable when I read it on my couch one evening, three children snug in their beds.[2] I programmed an alarm on my phone to buzz at noon.

By lunchtime the next day, the alarm chimed an annoying West-minster Abbey–like tune that I was quite sure I wouldn't have cho-sen unless I had known this was going to be a short-term thing. Flustered confusion tore my attention in pieces between the burner where macaroni was boiling over, the crying child on the floor, and shutting off that *blessed* chime.

A devotion and a song were not the things coming out of my mouth.

Instead we sang "Thank You, Jesus" and blessed our macaroni. As usual. This is simply the reality of this season, when most of my kids can count their ages on one hand. And yet their devotion and song can't be the high-water mark of my own time with God. Someday the kids will move out (this is my hope), and then what will we have left, Dave and I? Is it enough to invest solely in our kids' faith? I don't think so.

Prior to this year of small things, Dave and I had no shared faith practices outside of worshiping together on Sundays. In November, we set out to change that: we promised to meet each night at ten o'clock to pray.

Now, we could have chosen to fast, or practice solitude, or any number of spiritual disciplines that gurus like Richard Fos-ter encourage us to pursue in our quest for holiness. And, to be clear, we haven't entirely neglected the other disciplines this year. For example, we'll explore keeping the Sabbath when we discuss time in chapter 6; and simplicity—the hallmark of chapters 3 and 5—is at heart a spiritual endeavor. But for this month, it's one small thing, one tiny practice, perhaps the least heroic and most obvious: prayer.

This was our attempt to make the sixth and twelfth marks of new monasticism ("intentional formation in the way of Christ and the rule of the community along the lines of the old novitiate" and "commitment to a disciplined contemplative life") doable in our context, which doesn't often offer a lot of free time for contemplation.

That I moved in overnight with Dave in college but took almost a decade to find the courage to pray aloud with this man reveals a place on our relationship map where I would have written, "There be monsters." This entire region—praying together, without children to deflect awkwardness—was a featureless, unexplored area, our newest frontier.

When I think about people I know who are great at prayer, my grandparents and my children rise to the top. Dave and I don't even register. I prefer my thoughts on prayer to focus either on long-standing faith or wide-eyed confidence in the man named Jesus.

The rosary was my grandparents' prayer of choice. Grandma would show up before Mass to join other women who prayed that Catholic series of prayers; my mom remembers car rides and family nights spent moving beads between fingers and thumbs and reciting beautiful, old prayers. Once, after a car accident that totaled their Oldsmobile, Grandma asked the sheriff's deputy if she could crawl back inside to get the beads from her rosary, which she'd been praying. The string had broken, and she collected the beads into a plastic bag to take home. Now, in the end stages of Alzheimer's, she's long since stopped praying the words herself. But in November, while my daughter read to her from a children's book in the common area of the nursing center in Ohio, I noticed Grandma's thumb making the motion of advancing a rosary bead.

So when it comes to the spiritual discipline of prayer, I think of my grandmother; but I also think of my new tribe, all these kids. Since our oldest was a toddler, we've been intentional about the spiritual words and traditions we wanted to give the girls: we recite Bible verses from index cards while we eat oatmeal; we pray before meals and on the couch together after baths. My youngest stammers through the Lord's Prayer with the confidence of, well, a child.

Sandwiched between the rich faith of my grandparents and the practices we've put in place for our girls, though, has been a desert.

The first few nights in this new wilderness were like lying on a patch of prairie without a mat, a cloudy sky overhead. I'd hoped to see the heavens; I saw, instead, a look of hesitation on Dave's face.

"You want to talk or should I?" he asked.

"I don't know. I can, I guess."

"Okay." We paused, cleared our throats, tugged at our own pajama sleeves, smoothed a blanket over our legs.

"Maybe we should start with *Common Prayer*." I opened the website on his phone's screen. I read aloud:

> Behold now, bless the LORD, all you servants of the LORD, you that stand by night in the house of the LORD.[3]

"I think we're doing it right," I joked the first night, after we'd shared our petitions, prayed the Our Father, and met each other's eyes, wide open in self-awareness as we stumbled through the daily devotions for "At the Close of Day." ("I think I read this line, and you respond with this one." We'd read each other's lines accidentally. "Why don't you just read it all the way through?" "This part's your part.")

Light beams did not emanate from our fingertips.

But we survived. And we did it again the next night, and most nights since. Surprisingly, blessedly, this is the one practice within this whole year that we've nailed from the start—after those initial nights of awkwardness.

Nothing in my Catholic confirmation class prepared me for this work. Instead, meeting each night has turned what felt weird and forced into something I look forward to at the end of the day. We've become more loquacious in our petitions: praying for our family, our children, and our church. We pray more confidently now about parenthood and our careers, about rooting ourselves in a neighborhood. We pray, always, for patience in all these things, reminding each other and ourselves that change takes time. Small things.

This is, as Lauren Winner writes, "painting the middle tint," painting the parts of the masterpiece that don't immediately capture our attention.[4] The earth beneath us doesn't quake with delight; our words aren't sexy. What we're doing, though, is creating a ritual of being close, praying aloud, and pointing each other toward God.

•○•○•

In the third, fourth, and fifth centuries, a contingent of lay Christians headed to the desert for a life marked by simplicity, poverty, charity, stability, and prayer. All their lives, the desert fathers and mothers practiced Paul's command to pray without ceasing (see 1 Thess. 5:17). Most of the other Christian practices leave room for rest, Father Agatho said, "but we need to pray till our dying breath. That is the greatest struggle."[5]

One little detail causes me to raise my hand here: these desert parents *weren't actually parents*. Agatho, I'll see that "greatest struggle" and raise you a husband, three children, potty training, lost winter gloves, four rounds of amoxicillin, and a dog.

But we can do this in community. That's why, on Tuesday nights this month, the Arthurs and the Wasingers instituted one other small thing: closing our weekly gatherings with a simple prayer circle. So how does this work? Well, remember, the oldest child was six when we began; you must remember this, or everything that follows will be unremarkable.

The first night we prayed together in the Arthurs' living room, someone flipped off the lights. In the parsonage's open floor plan, the effect was immediate. Children froze; sounds halted. Something different was happening, they knew, because for weeks before this, our Tuesday meals had ended in craziness. Stuffed animals went flying. Children wailed or ran in circles. They sneezed in each other's faces and fought over a guitar. At least one child ate Tums from all the stress. (Maybe our lofty theological reasons for implementing communal prayer were less important than needing to catch our breaths.)

This time, in the darkened room, attentions were refocused to a flickering flame in a votive, placed gently on the carpet. Everyone was invited to sit around the candle and calm his or her body—and to keep back from the candle. "Please, let's all move back from the candle," Sarah repeated, over and over. (In any other monastic setting, this could count as a liturgy—say, the Litany of Real Fire for Small Folks.)

God only knows how spiritual our inner monologues actually were when our main focus was on keeping a four-year-old's stuffed animal away from the flame, but the allure of that candle signaled this was a holy moment in our frenetic day. Our heart rates slowed as we asked one another two simple questions, modified from what is known as the Ignatian Examen: "What made you happy this week?" and "What made you sad?"[6] As each parent or child shared her or his thoughts in turn, an adult responded simply with "Thank you, God, for friends and pizza," or "God, please be with us when we don't want to clean up." "Yes, God, thank you for Mr. Big." "Micah, please keep Huckle away from the flame." (Huckle the stuffed dog always has a spot in the prayer circle—just another reason that it took us less than three weeks to dig out a flameless candle.)

Ever since that first night, each week we end with the Lord's Prayer and sing "Go Now in Peace" as we don our coats and collect leftovers from dinner. We wave good-bye on the porch, go home, and put on pajamas. It's a benediction for our week that makes bedtime smooth, sure. But more fruitful has been the creation of a spiritually formative community there on Tuesdays. We four adults are teaching our five kids that spiritual stuff is just part of life; it's normal.

It's a privilege to share this covenantal ritual. For one, the Arthurs use a different spiritual language. My children experience a richer understanding of prayer when I'm not the only adult praying with them. They learn that prayer isn't solely private and that it takes many forms. They learn that it's normal to pray with other people, aloud. They find their voices too.

On a larger scale, the model we employ on Tuesdays is strong not only because it's simple but also because it's a reinforcement of what we do at church. Every Sunday at SCC, our children and teenagers spend part of their time together reflecting on those same two questions and then praying the Lord's Prayer with their peers. This is by design, as Sarah and I introduced that pattern both to give our children continued chances to practice the formative language and rituals of their spiritual heritage and to foster community among the families at church. So, really, at any home after a potluck or party, our church's families could do this with one another and it wouldn't be weird. It's now the mother tongue of our children's spiritual life.

And it goes on: six nights out of the week, Dave and I gather at eight o'clock on the couch to ask our three girls about their days and pray. Grandparents recite this simple liturgy with our kids on overnight trips, and when they don't, our children begin it themselves and rebuke Grandma for going off-script.

You might say we're making the smallest, cutest novitiate monks.

Sarah's Story

When Erin and Dave, that Tuesday night at dinner, shyly made their big announcement (like cute newlyweds trying for a baby: "We're praying together! Every night!"), Tom and I glanced at each other. There. That's what we had needed: the simple reminder to keep the whole spiritual practices thing, well, simple.

Because this is one area where the former "temple"—which in our minds had grown in impressiveness and glory—completely eclipsed anything we had attempted to create since.

At Isaiah House we had prayed almost daily in community: evening and sometimes morning prayer, complete with candles, Taizé chants on CD, various experiments with liturgy, you name it (except the sacraments; those were for church). Occasionally we took spiritual retreats together or set aside a day for study and prayer. One year during Lent we practiced silence on Wednesdays from the moment evening prayer ended to the start of breakfast the next day, with relative success. Meanwhile, Tom and I also attended morning prayer in the seminary chapel most days for several years.

Note: when left to my own devices, this is not generally how I roll. Various failed attempts at regular spiritual disciplines in high school, college, and young adulthood eventually petered out into self-defeating guilt. When it finally occurred to me that the hyper-religious phrase "personal quiet time," whatever that means, was not in the Bible, I exhaled with relief and started writing poetry instead.

By contrast, I'm married to one of the most natural, unaffected pietists you'll ever meet. This is a man who knows in his bones that if you don't build regular spiritual habits into your daily life, they won't happen—and your soul will shrink. Yes, the Holy Spirit shows up in your everyday life sometimes, even in powerful ways, offering inspiration and emotional highs, but in the meantime, you make a commitment and stick to it. It's how we grow in grace—sanctification, if you will. So from the time he was a teenager, my husband has been building regular personal and communal spiritual practices into his life: solo prayer and Bible study (yes, "quiet time") most mornings; small groups for accountability and encouragement; spiritual retreats on a regular basis; fasting in some form every week or month; praying at noon with his staff at church; the list goes on.

Which, apart from grace, makes someone like me feel like a loser. All. The. Time. So community saved me—saved us—you might say. Daily devotions with my family as a child and teenager—*that* I could do. Student-led prayer services in the chapel at seminary—*that* I could do. Morning and evening prayer with my husband and Isaiah House—boom.

Then came the move to our single-family household in Lansing, quickly followed by baby number one. And it all fell apart. And when I say "all," I mean *all*. No more evening prayer together. ("Evening?" says the nursing mom of a newborn. "When's that?")

No more "personal quiet time"; now Tom was writing in an anger journal, battling paternal postpartum depression. When we sat down for dinner, we couldn't even muster words of our own. We used the prayer cube, reading in flat, sleep-deprived tones asking for God to . . . verb . . . object . . . something or other. Finally, baby number two did us in.

But now, in this year of small things, maybe the Wasingers were on to something. Maybe it really was that small, that simple. Earlier that year Tom and I had attempted to institute the 10:00 p.m. rule: that's when the laptops and tablets would close and we'd head to bed. We were already sleep-deprived, so we didn't need for our jobs to suck the last remaining life from our numb brains. Ten o'clock: done. And it worked, sort of. But what if, after closing our screens, we met in bed with our worn, dusty copies of the *Book of Common Prayer*? (When was the last time I had even picked it up? I couldn't remember.) Just one page, 140: "Daily devotions at the close of the day." That's all. Not "Evening Prayer: Rite Two," complete with full lessons from the Old and New Testaments, chanting the psalm by half verse, all those canticles, suffrages, and collects, plus a Taizé chant thrown in there because it's cool. Nope. Just one page.

One small thing.

Could we?

The short answer is yes. Mostly. Many nights. We're getting there, anyway, almost a year into it. It's not the glorious temple of our past, lit up with flames and billowing with incense. But it's the call we're answering right now.

Amazing how motivated you are to stick with something when two friends look at you across the dinner table and ask, "How is prayer together going?"

Back to Erin

So. You should know about the midyear lull, if you're going to commit to this experiment.

When we vowed in November to add the spiritual discipline of prayer to our days, it was a mere four months into our cumulative year. Momentum was high. Friendships were forming. Winter had just practiced with an eight-inch snowfall. Everything felt fresh, new, and lovely.

By March, however, I could see how the earlier work we had done to tone our spiritual muscles was necessary to see us through the tougher times. The desert fathers had their desert; we have Michigan winters.

So often, the fruit of all these months felt too small, or we'd stall out on a practice we'd begun with zeal. (This can happen. Expect it.) Tom would remind us that, if he were the author, he'd write *The Year of Big Things*, because we weren't always great at hitting the small stuff. Maybe the problem was the size of our targets. While loading a dishwasher together, we'd acknowledge that we looked little like the powerful examples given by all those new monastics—let alone Jesus—and not for lack of desire. Or maybe it's that no one else was writing about how damp towels and mismatched toddler socks pile up by the washing machine, and this does not stop. Children start sniffling. Mufflers rust away. Sunday-school planning beckons. The dog gets fleas.

It's often difficult to see what God's doing when it feels like the ordinary things such as ear infections and tax bills are arguments for why new monasticism can't work in our context. To wit: In October, Dave's job was in limbo during a reorganization at the newspaper. He got a new role there in November, around Thanksgiving, and our single-income family exhaled.

And still, each week, we meet and talk. But more importantly, we pause and pray. "Erin, what made you sad this week?" "I'm sad that Lou's ears hurt." "God, help LouLou feel better. Please fix her ears." We pray to the God who saves us from thinking we can do any of this on our own neat timetable or by the powers of our own imaginations. God blesses our year of small things through community and provision, but God also probably thinks it's cute that we attempted to map out where the Holy Spirit would be moving.

This time with God reminds us that we're beloved, mysteriously, no matter how few marks we hit this year.

•••••

So what does this mean for you? The first step, of course, is just to begin.

In solitude, begin. (Yes, even you moms. Susanna Wesley, eighteenth-century mother of the famous John and Charles—plus something like twenty other children—is said to have pulled the hem of her apron up over her face to pray, and the kids knew not to disturb her.) Breathe in and out the simple words of the ancient prayer, "Lord, have mercy on me, a sinner"—and if you can't get that out before a small, grubby person finds you hiding in the bathroom, break it down to just "Lord, have mercy."

In your most intimate relationships, begin. With your spouse, meet in bed or at breakfast to follow a pattern of prayer so ancient it predates channel surfing by a couple thousand years. With children, sit on the floor with a story Bible and tell God what you wonder about it. Carving out the time and creating the routine is work, but it's work that each time brings you in direct conversation with the creator of the universe. It's kind of a big deal.

Now draw your family circle a little wider; extend it to your church. Whose lives around you radiate God's presence? Whose lives need it? Invite them. Perhaps it's your covenantal friendship; maybe it's a small group that closes out each weekend with a potluck and sharing prayer requests. Maybe it's colleagues who work in proximity to each other, grabbing the morning's first cup of coffee to pray through *Common Prayer* with other "ordinary radicals."[7]

People sought the desert fathers for advice on holiness; there's no shame in not knowing where to begin. Call a mentor. Buy a book (we've listed several at the end of this chapter). Start in the book of Psalms, "the great school of prayer."[8] Read them with someone else to enliven your imagination to the ways in which they're prayers of a people, not just of an individual, using the language of God.

For those in church leadership, especially in nontraditional contexts, creating a simple routine for prayer within our spheres of influence (and in conversation with those with whom we work and worship) can be grounding, particularly when others take ownership of those routines and use them for themselves. As we've described, Sycamore Creek Church spins off Saint Ignatius's daily *examen* by asking about highs and lows. It can happen in staff meetings, in small groups, or just over coffee with a friend.

Mine your faith tradition, or the traditions of our spiritual ancestors, for practices worth adapting. Experiment with other spiritual disciplines within a community, whether it be celebration, fasting, confession, service, or another unfamiliar or forgotten practice. Feed yourself in solitude; feed your tribe in community. Grant grace.

Yes, this is often unsexy, boring work—we memorize words by rote; we find ourselves on autopilot on occasion. But if the crux of the entire year of small things—nay, a life of faith—rests on listening and discerning, we ought to acquire the habit of stillness and attune the ear to hear God's voice. And no longer alone, but within the daily, weekly accountability of the shared Christian life.

~~~~~~ *Questions for Reflection and Discussion* ~~~~~~

1. How do your church's practices and liturgies shape your own spiritual life?

2. How do you see Paul's advice to "pray without ceasing" (1 Thess. 5:17) playing out in your context? What does that

look like in singleness? With a spouse? With children (young, teens, or otherwise)?

3. In what ways could your community or covenantal friend-ships provide accountability for your practice of spiritual disciplines?

~~~~~ *For Further Reading* ~~~~~~~~~~~~~~~~~~~~~~~~~

Borgo, Lacy Finn, and Ben Barczi. *Good Dirt: Devotionals for the Spiritual Formation of Families*. Vols. 1–3. N.p.: CreateSpace, 2014.

Claiborne, Shane, Jonathan Wilson-Hartgrove, and Enuma Okoro. *Common Prayer: A Liturgy for Ordinary Radicals*. Grand Rapids: Zondervan, 2010.

Foster, Nathan. *The Making of an Ordinary Saint: My Journey from Frus-tration to Joy with the Spiritual Disciplines*. Grand Rapids: Baker Books, 2014.

Winner, Lauren F. *Still: Notes from a Mid-faith Crisis*. New York: Harper-One, 2012.

5

stuff

Celebration brings joys into life, and joy makes us strong.

—Richard Foster[1]

Erin's Story

On Christmas Day, while Dave and I watched in our pajamas, Alice tore the brown-paper wrapping off a stuffed dinosaur, new colored pencils, and a used copy of *The Railway Children*. A month's worth of planning and preparation over in forty-five, maybe sixty seconds. Her eyes darted to her sisters' hauls: Violet held up the bunk bed curtains I sewed (in the hopes she'd sleep past dawn), markers, and *Imogene's Antlers*; Lou opened the clothespin people I'd painted, an Elmo doll, and *Poems to Read to Young Children*.

"Is this all the presents?" one of my footed pajama–clad children asked.

Dangerous pause.

"Hey, what do you guys say?" Dave prompted them, eyeing my plastered-on smile. (I rarely smile before ten in the morning, so it really was plaster.)

"Thank you, Mom, for making my dinosaur," Alice said dutifully, in that singsong voice children reserve for well-practiced, fake gratitude. Then she tried to console her sisters: "Hey, here's a good thing: we get to open more presents tomorrow at Grandma and Grandpa's, and then more at Nina and Poppy's house in three days. Then we get more presents at Grandpa Niese's!"

Bad news: I've given birth to human beings, not angels.

•••••

Twenty-five bucks for gifts; a hundred to give away. That was our challenge this December, when our new monastic adventures in simplicity led us to focus on "stuff." Not twenty-five bucks per person, but twenty-five *total*.

Game on, to quote the Arthurs.

The Wasingers—champs in the thrift-store circuit, used-book aficionados, and crafty geniuses that we are—chose to freak out the grandparents by putting a crazy-low dollar amount on our Christmas spending. "We're going to be making a lot of our gifts so we can give more away to our church missions and a couple of other projects," we enthusiastically, emphatically repeated to our kids, their grandparents, and other skeptics. We shopped for an adopt-a-family, we budgeted to give cash at Sycamore Creek's Christmas Eve offering, and we spent more time bringing cheer—caroling, sending cards—instead of buying it.

(A certain set of grandparents, by the way, took this to mean they must step up their gift-buying to compensate. "I don't do simplicity," one grandparent said. "And you can put that in your book.")

We get it; this year of small things is weird to other people. If you choose to tackle "stuff" around December, be prepared. Gift exchanges may smell a lot more like homemade cinnamon granola and a lot less like the mall (whatever that smells like). And you may get the distinct impression, from little and big people alike, that you're not their favorite person.

When Sarah and I sketched out this year on a legal pad, we split the basic practice of simplicity into two parts: money and stuff. We listed "money" in October, as early in the experiment as we could, because finances can be the biggest obstacle to a life of radical faith. And we chose to tackle "stuff" in December because, hello, the holidays. If we're honest with ourselves, stuff gets in the way of the marks of living a contemplative life. Simplicity is a discipline, after all, and the burden of excess stuff can be the manifestation of chaos, complexity. While much of the developing world struggles to feed and clothe and provide for its children, many parents in the United States face the absurdly first-world problem of LEGO pieces, too many of them, painfully crunching under our bare feet as we tiptoe to the closet in the dark to find that overflowing bin of Santa wrapping paper—so we can put even more LEGO sets under the Christmas tree. *Stuff* is how Americans are, on the whole, undisciplined. Clear out the clutter and you can make room for Jesus.

The tension is in ensuring we're not mistaking a less cluttered, more affordable Christmas for a cheerless one. How would we celebrate without stuff being the focus? Christmas is our holiday, after all, we Christians. It's a joyful pause right at winter's beginning. It's our chance to *increase* our giving to our community and the poor—to live into the second mark of new monasticism, which is about "sharing economic resources." It's appropriate and wonderful for us to celebrate with gifts to our friends and family. The gifts are tangible reminders that we follow a God who is known for giving good gifts—all of them, actually (see James 1:17).

The otherwise verbose apostle Paul never got around to writing about the annual Christmas party in any of his New Testament epistles.[2] So how we celebrate as American Christians is influenced

almost exclusively by our culture.³ Rather than asking ourselves
to abstain from joy, I ask instead, how could we redeem this?
While we might be retroactively dictating how we celebrate what
has become a secular affair, perhaps we Christians can stake our
celebrations on more than stuff. We can turn its excess into abun-
dance for those in need; we can celebrate God's story.

Celebration, after all, is holy work. For example, the jovial
Jewish holiday of Purim exists because of a command at the
end of the book of Esther. The Jews are to remember "the time
when the Jews got relief from their enemies"—in this case, the
evil Haman's plot to wipe out the entire Jewish community in
Persia—"and as the month when their sorrow was turned into
joy and their mourning into a day of celebration. [Esther's uncle,
Mordecai] wrote them to observe the days as days of feasting and
joy and giving presents of food to one another and gifts to the
poor" (Esther 9:22 NIV). If ever there was such a thing as a holy
kegger, this is it. And the gifts are an integral part of remembering what God has done—not just gifts to one another but to the
poor as well.

Likewise, at Christmas we can do the same thing: we give and
we remember God's victories. There's no biblical mandate that we
do this—unless you count the commands to care for the poor, the
orphans, the widows among us⁴—but as you make those responsible budgets, bake granola, string beads on a necklace, or (if you
must) shop, turn your thoughts back to the story of redemption.
The process should be refining to our souls; the anticipation and
joy of giving someone a gift should bring us closer to the One
who gives good gifts. If we're focused only on the deliverables,
we miss the chance to see gift giving as a process of our ongoing
sanctification. That's what the spiritual disciplines are for, after
all: forming us more and more into the image of Christ, who is
both the ultimate Gift and the ultimate Giver.

•••••

Don't worry; I'm human too. My sanctification was not the first thing on my mind around December twentieth, when I had a child with an ear infection crying out at one in the morning for an Elmo doll that I'd given to Goodwill. *Of all the stupid things.* "So I bought another Elmo doll for her for Christmas," I confessed to the Arthurs later. In my defense, the new one was smaller and didn't sing.

"That's okay," Sarah said. "We were at the thrift store last week to buy pajamas, in an effort to live more simply. And of the hundreds of books there, Micah found one of his that I'd donated last month . . . in an effort to live more simply. It was ten cents. I mean, c'mon."

Of all the stupid things. And there are a lot of stupid things.

Keeping your sense of humor is a spiritual discipline too, right?

●●◆●●

We talked a lot in December about the toll of a stringent budget. It's hard work. The dollar limit dragged me back again and again to my calculator, which never brings me joy. Whereas another person could have found creative passion in the boundary of a healthy budget, I took it to its legalistic breaking point. In the end our family still wound up talking way too much about stuff, way too little about Jesus. Next year, I finally conceded, we're doing it differently.

Thankfully, the community offers us grace. And it's not just at Christmas, of course, that we're challenging one another to live simply and practice the discipline of celebration. To be honest, I find celebration difficult. ("That's why it's a Christian *discipline*," Tom loves to point out. "*Thanks*, resident pietist," I reply.) So I have to practice this thing. A lot. We play out the holy drama of simplicity and celebration all year, Tuesday after Tuesday. We admit when we feel less than joyful; we talk about the things we want, the gifts we're considering, the ways we're celebrating. We pray, and we bake. Sarah made me pie when I preached; Dave baked scones for the Arthurs because—actually, I don't know why. We can celebrate just for the joy of it.

And yet, even those of us with long experience in both celebration and budgetary simplicity find outside forces pressing in at Christmastime.

Sarah's Story

Various circumstances conspired to make this the Year of Too Many Things. For starters, Tom's mom and stepdad downsized from two houses to one, and on their summer trip to Lansing, right as our year of small things began, they brought a carload of stuff from Indianapolis.

Additionally, we still owned our house in Petoskey, the one we'd had since we were newlyweds. You remember the guy to whom we had offered hospitality all those years ago? More than a decade later, he still lived there as a renter downstairs, while we had the upstairs to enjoy when we were in town. And the arrangement had worked nicely until recently, when his health had begun to fail, keeping him from work, which kept him from paying rent. We went months and months without it, actually, all during this year of small things. While our family budget got tighter and tighter, and Micah's feet got bigger and bigger, and Sam had yet another sinus infection, all those Petoskey bills kept coming in. But, we told ourselves, our renter was old, and sick, and it was his home. He had lived there longer than we had.

"Radical hospitality run amok," Erin jokingly, lovingly called it. But, you know? I just couldn't kick Jesus out of my house.

Eventually—through those weekly dinners with our wise friends, who were praying—it became clear that staying there was not the best, healthiest thing for him, or for us. We had begun to realize that it was probably time to sell the house altogether. So we gave Jesus till May.

You think I jest. But really, we put this in God's hands. Or rather, *Tom* put it in God's hands, while I fretted and stewed and worried. What would happen? The house needed what I felt was tons of work, much of which we couldn't do till our renter moved out. And meanwhile, the *stuff*. It was an entire furnished household, after all. Beds, tables, bookshelves, dishes, towels, even a grill. Not to mention, over the years the Petoskey house had become a kind of storage unit for all the memorabilia we hadn't wanted to drag around. (Where do new monastics keep their high school yearbooks?)

"We pray for wisdom about the Petoskey house," Tom would say during our 10:00 p.m. prayer times. I'd bite my nails.

"What do we *do*?" I'd wail at our Tuesday dinners, Erin and Dave nodding patiently. "This is Jesus we're talking about. I can't kick him out."

Over the fall months, we made several visits up north, taking both cars so we could load up as much as possible and bring it home. And with each new carload came a new wave of guilt, another round of doubts about whether we were doing the right thing.

And more stuff.

We piled it in the basement, hauled it to thrift stores, gave it away. By the beginning of Advent, I had started avoiding going downstairs altogether.

In short, we no longer owned stuff. It owned us.

That's about when Tom decided we had to make a preemptive strike against the inevitable accumulation of even more. Christmas loomed, threatening an avalanche. We had to stop this madness. Now.

"We need to write a letter," Tom declared at our weekly Tuesday dinner. "We need to write to our extended family, asking them to give to SCC's Christmas Eve offering instead of giving to us."

"But—" a small voice wobbled from the kid's table. Tom hadn't realized Micah was listening. "But what about . . ." Tears shimmered in Micah's sad blue eyes.

"You mean," I said to Tom carefully, "they can still give the *boys* presents. Just not to you and me."

"Sure. One gift each to the boys," he said.

Micah blinked at Daddy, rubbing Huckle against his own cheek for comfort.

"And meanwhile we can *make* gifts," I said brightly. "That will be way more fun than buying a bunch of presents!"

Erin and Dave observed this tennis match, heads swiveling back and forth.

"Christmas," Tom said firmly, "is not *our* birthday."

"Agreed," I said. The letter sounded like a good idea, anyway.

"So. A letter," he said.

"Sure," I caved.

"I like it," Erin chimed in. "Can you give us a copy?"

So that was our one small thing in the practice of material simplicity for December: a letter emailed to all our extended family (see appendix C). And they responded graciously by honoring our requests. We still hadn't resolved what to do about the Petoskey house—that story will progress later. But at least we had put on the brakes. Stuff was not going to win.

Back to Erin

Maybe Christmas isn't the right time of year for you to tackle stuff. We get it. Good news: you can practice navigating between simplicity and celebration at any point. Remember, Jesus turned water into wine at a wedding (see John 2:1–11); this guy knows that celebration is healthy at any time of year. How can you celebrate the gifts God's given you—without those gifts ultimately owning you?

And it's not just about asking your children to live with fewer stuffed animals. (Sorry. That does sound blissful, doesn't it?) It may mean asking yourself how you are blessing your community by sharing the stuff you do have. Do you open for your community's use your tool shed or garage, your kids' clothes closets, your school supplies, your washer and dryer, your car?

If you've got the nagging feeling that you have too much stuff, start there. Grab a box and tackle one room. Empty the spare room, then celebrate with a cup of tea. Then do the kitchen cupboards the next month. In a couple of months, do the garage if you've got one. When you clear the basement, celebrate. Hold a garage sale, or just give it all away. Then, most importantly, ask those in covenantal friendship to check in with you about it so you don't use the extra space to store more stuff. (Ask someone to move in; that'll limit your free space.)

Look outward for support. How can your church hold you accountable and challenge you to share more—financially or with gear, clothes, spare bedrooms, whatever you have? Ask your small group or your covenantal friendships to ask you the hard questions before big purchases or holidays; ask one another how you might meet one another's needs without buying more stuff. (Consider: I was a Michigander with no winter boots. I was remarking to Sarah one Tuesday that my socks were soaked after a recent trudge through the snow. "You don't have boots?" She was incredulous. "Goodwill never has my size," I said. She disappeared to the closet, emerging with a pair. A pair exactly my size. "Use mine," she said. "I have two.")

Make it easy for others to know what stuff you have. At Sycamore Creek Church, we have a "Stuff" sheet in our directory. If we're going camping, I know a couple who has a tent we can borrow. If Dave wants to can tomatoes, the Arthurs have the gear. Dave made a table last year using a fellow parishioner's saw. We remind one another that God meets our needs when we pool our resources for the sake of the community.

•••••

Once again, we circle back to Sycamore Creek Church. It was the long-awaited Christmas Eve. There in the candlelit sanctuary,

my frenzied soul finally paused. It was held in the near-darkness
by Marian's voice, belting out Beyoncé's version of "Ave Maria."

This was the kind of moment when remembering strikes. It wasn't
the gift prep that did it, in the end. While there was nothing intrinsi-
cally good or bad about the twenty-five-dollar cap on our spending,
I had focused so much on the legalism that I missed the joy, the sanctification. Marian sang me back to the meaning of the gift giving.
And this is what the church can do: the church can bear powerful,
steadfast witness that the story is louder than the culture. The church
can remind us with the same carols, the same Bible stories, the same
themes every year, year after year. It can show us both the Gift and
the Giver, that in spite of us and all our fumblings, there is hope,
that we're part of this redemptive work now.

Tom reminds us each Christmas Eve what God is up to in our
little Lansing congregation, through the medical mission in Nicaragua that we've supported for more than a decade. But this
year we were being given the chance to support not just our doctor friend's ministry but also a local charity and the Imagine No
Malaria campaign. Tom told these stories again now, invited us
into something bigger. And then he asked us to give.

I sat there, the money we'd set aside for the offering in my
purse. And then I remembered another bill—the good kind, the
money kind, not the debtor kind—in my purse from a night I'd
babysat for someone's child in a pinch. "I found heaven on earth,
/ You are my last, my first," Marian sang, the rest of us in awe
of her talent. "And then I hear this voice inside . . ."

"Give it too," I heard then. Not audibly, but my kingdom-
hungry mind was captured by the beauty of Marian's vocals and
the vision of being part of God's redemption plan.

"What are you doing?" Dave whispered.

I shrugged. "I just thought I should."

That's why we do a minimalist Christmas; that's why we give
away more than we spend on ourselves. We may have fumbled this
year, but we'll keep trying.

~~~~~~ *Questions for Reflection and Discussion* ~~~~~~~~

1. Would you say that you own stuff or that stuff owns you?
2. Especially around the holidays or birthdays, how easy or difficult is it for you to balance celebration and simplicity? Why?
3. Are you talking about simplicity with your closest family members, especially when it comes to stuff? If so, what does that look like? If not, how could you begin?
4. How could your church or neighborhood encourage the sharing of resources with the community?
5. In what ways are you hoping to grow in the practice of living simply over the next months?

~~~~~~ *For Further Reading* ~~~~~~~~~~~~~~~~~~~~~~~~~~

Foster, Richard J. *The Freedom of Simplicity: Finding Harmony in a Complex World*. New York: HarperCollins, 1981.

Hatmaker, Jen. *7: An Experimental Mutiny against Excess*. Nashville: B&H, 2012.

Samson, Will, and Lisa Samson. *Enough: Contentment in an Age of Excess*. Colorado Springs: David C. Cook, 2009.

6

holy time

How strange to use the most airtime [at Mount Sinai]
on the Sabbath command.

—Walter Brueggemann[1]

Sarah's Story

"Are you sure they know we're coming?" I peered through fogged
car windows at the dripping woods as Tom navigated the slushy,
icy entrance to a camp in northern Michigan. Two days after
Christmas, the denominational retreat center looked deserted.

"Yep," Tom said. "I was told the cabin would be open and the
heat on—and there should be firewood stacked somewhere."

It started to rain as the car skated down the last hill. We wound
our way past the shuttered bunkhouses and pulled up next to a
snug little cabin in a stand of pines. Thanks to an odd midwinter
thaw, this was not exactly the North Woods escape we'd hoped

for; snowshoeing in deep powder wouldn't be on the agenda after
all. But the minute I glimpsed our tiny getaway, I exhaled, long
and slow.

Two days. No kids. Just Tom and me, a bag of foodie-lovers'
groceries, a quaint log cabin, and a pile of books.

Time to breathe. Time to sleep if I wanted to. Time to eat at
my own pace, read whatever I chose. Hours and hours to scribble
reflections in a notebook and tromp through the slush down to the
frozen lake. Inhale, exhale, make peace with myself and creation.

We unpacked the car, settled in. I curled up on the couch by
the fire, content to simply stare out the window in the silence for
a while.

Silence . . . When was the last time . . . ? I couldn't even . . .

Then Tom said, "So. Here's what I'm thinking."

I should have known better than to go on a spiritual retreat
with a pietist. The word "relax" is not in his vocabulary—unless
it's on the schedule under "practice Sabbath rest for one hour."
John Wesley, you've got nothing on this guy.

I barely controlled the aggrieved eye rolling I had once per-
fected as an artsy teenager and turned a blank face in his direction. "Yes?"

But I knew what was coming. Tom had an agenda for this spiritual retreat. Otherwise, in his mind, it didn't qualify as a *spiritual*
retreat; it was just a getaway, and anyone can get away. On some
level he's right: if you don't build spiritual habits into your life,
they don't just happen. But the poet in me shrank a little. Please,
couldn't we just have a little unscheduled time? Time for my soul
to expand? Time for my shoulder muscles to unclench? Time for
my brain to do that subconscious thing it does right before it has
a creative breakthrough?

And yet I didn't go on that retreat alone. I came at Tom's
invitation, because he wanted to share his quarterly spiritual
retreat with me. (Granted, sex was also an undisguised bonus,
in his mind—and no, Tom and Dave, this is not the chapter on

sex. There is no chapter on sex.) I was there, as I am in the rest of life, with a pietist. And if I've learned nothing else in eighteen years of marriage, it's that we're happiest after we've negotiated the schedule.

"So," he said slowly, sensing my resistance, "I'm thinking for the next few hours we rest in silence or read, or whatever you want to do."

"Great."

"Then maybe a hike together?"

"Sure."

"Then we make dinner."

"Okay."

"And then after dinner I have this year-end-review document that I thought we could each fill out and discuss."

Pause. Stony, mutinous silence from the couch.

He pressed on. "It's just one page, with questions about how things went in different areas of your life last year —you know, emotional, spiritual, relational—and what you hope this year will be like."

I glanced at the paper in his hand. "That's two-sided," I said, eyes narrowing.

"One page," he said firmly.

Deep, annoyed sigh. I would not win this skirmish, and we both knew it.

"Fine," I said with quiet, Teen-Martyr-Faces-Adult-Tigers bravery. Let the pietists take the field once again. Blame them if there's no artistic beauty in the world. Or poetry. I'd done my best.

•••••

Several restful hours, a long hike, and a leisurely meal later, we were back in front of the fire filling out the dreaded year-end review. And here's the thing: it wasn't that bad. The overachiever in me warmed up as I started filling empty spaces under "Am I closer to God than I was last year?" and "Are my finances in order?" It was almost—and I can't believe I'm acknowledging this—fun.

But when, under the section "Emotional Health," I read, "Where is there clutter in my life?" I paused.

Emotional clutter? It wasn't a phrase I'd come across before. But it rang true. Yes, my physical existence felt like an epic battle against "stuff," as Erin and I described last month. But so did my mental/emotional existence—especially as it played out in my schedule. Or in the way I filled my time, which was not always the same as what was on my calendar (more on that in a moment). In short, there was clutter everywhere.

Earlier on that vacation, I had spent the entire drive from Lansing to the North Woods listening to the audiobook version of *All Joy and No Fun: The Paradox of Modern Parenting* by Jennifer Senior. I had, by turns, nodded in recognition and gasped, appalled, at what modern parents are doing to themselves. It was as if she was filming in Technicolor what David Robinson warns against in his beautiful, quiet book *The Busy Family's Guide to Spirituality*—namely, that if we do not create an intentional spiritual blueprint for our family life, external forces will dictate everything.[2] *Everything.* But especially our schedules.

Biblical mandates for Sabbath rest aside (and trust me, we'll come back to those), there are two key marks of new monasticism that speak to creating an intentional spiritual blueprint. The first we covered significantly in chapter 4: "intentional formation in the way of Christ and the rule of the community along the lines of the old novitiate." The second sounds very similar and is at first difficult to tease out from the first: the "commitment to a disciplined contemplative life." This is specifically about the individuals in the community, who each commit to time with God. But it has to be a communal discipline for it to work. If someone in the community sets aside Tuesday afternoons as his or her Sabbath, for instance, then everyone respects that person's commitment.

Here's the problem: it's one thing to individually commit to a disciplined contemplative life within a community of grownups; it's another to commit to it with children. As other parents have no doubt discovered, there is no Sabbath from parenting. Um, radical Christians, any thoughts on who will watch the kids while I take my quarterly spiritual retreat? Anyone? And yes, I know that the right answer is "the community," but the sheer acrobatics of making it all work with Tom's schedule, much less bringing the Wasingers and my entire church family into the mix, sounds like it could suck out my soul. I swear, if I have to organize *one more thing* . . .

I imagine it's the same tension a Jewish mother might feel as Friday evening approaches. The sun goes down and Sabbath begins, and her brain is running like a gerbil on a wheel. Have I cooked enough to feed these endlessly hungry children while I supposedly rest tomorrow? Do I wait to deal with this dirty diaper till sundown on Saturday? Doesn't anyone get how these little people need me? How the world needs me? How I am, in fact, indispensable?

Into this mix comes the God of Sabbath, who looks at his dear daughter flapping around the laundry room and says, "Peace, be still."

It's risky, this resting business. As theologian Walter Brueggemann suggests in his frank little book *Sabbath as Resistance*, to rest means to resist anxiety—anxiety that you're not adding up, not succeeding, not achieving, not accumulating, or worse: that you're making more work for yourself later.[3] To rest is to duel with that anxiety bare-handed, to beat back the demands of a ravenous consumer culture that will devour your family and your community and your church until there isn't a tiny crumb left for the Holy Spirit. It's to admit that these little people, including the nursing infant at your breast, don't need you. That God doesn't need you. That the world already has a Savior.[4]

Brueggemann compares our current craziness to the enslaved Israelites under Pharaoh, the dictator whose "endlessly anxious presence . . . caused the entire social environment to be permeated with a restless anxiety that had no limit or termination."⁵ Trade my name for Pharaoh's at the beginning of that description, and you could easily be describing me and the effect of all this anxiety on my poor children. God, by contrast, takes an entire day off from the act of creation (see Gen. 2:1–2). As Brueggemann puts it, "God absented God's self from the office. God did not come and check on creation in anxiety to be sure it was all working."⁶ Can I let it go, even for a few hours? Unclench the fist? Release my calendar? The answer isn't, "Sure, let's try it." It's, "You must." To my knowledge, the command to Sabbath rest (see Exod. 20:8–11) has never been rescinded.

This isn't merely about finding some kind of work/rest "balance." If anything, as Tom often reminds us, God seems to promote a kind of holy imbalance—otherwise, wouldn't there be equal parts rest and work? Instead, we work six days, we rest one. And yet, too often, we humans can't even manage that *one*.

We don't just rest because God rested—yes, that's a key theological point and a vital glimpse into God's own character and purpose. But, according to Deuteronomy 5:12–15, we also rest because we will not be slaves. Not to technology, not to soccer practice, not to our children, not to our own anxious selves. Not even, God help us, to the twelve small things we are trying to change this year.

And therein lies perhaps one of our biggest struggles. This year of small things has not made our lives any easier. Six months into it, we're faltering. Granted, it's winter, and we're the frazzled parents of a toddler and a preschooler, neither of whom can negotiate gloves unaided (Jesus, grant me patience). But, also, we've cumulatively added five things to our already full calendar: weekly dinner in community, welcoming a long-term guest into our household, getting cash envelopes for household expenses twice per month, praying as a couple every evening, and managing family expectations about our Christmas practices of simplicity—practices we want to continue, even after the holidays. Not surprisingly, our bursting schedules are fighting back.

These may be small changes, but add them all up, and they take big chunks of time.

It takes time, initially, talking and thinking and praying and reading and talking some more. Tom and I only have so many minutes together in a day (sometimes, technically, none); do we really want to be discussing the spiritual merits of cash versus debit? And then it takes time actually *doing* these new small things: Messaging the Wasingers on Monday to find out what they have in their pantry. Regularly making sure the guest bathroom has toilet paper. Pulling up at the bank window and getting cash from the chatty teller while shaking my head "no" when the bowl of lollipops appears. And so on. With just five new small things added to our daily lives, our schedules are more cluttered than ever.

And we have seven months to go.

If we're going to be serious about this—if these small things are not going to become merely our latest fad, a kind of hyperspiritual hobby that we try for a while and then drop—some other things will have to give. Soon. Now.

The question is, what? I could argue that everything on my calendar is necessary—indeed, even morally worthy. But let's be honest here: what's on my calendar is *not all* that I'm doing. We may not have a TV at the Arthur parsonage, but there are plenty of screens around to entertain the sleep-deprived parental brain—one of which I'm sitting in front of right now. And within three guesses I bet you can name what's on the next tab over from this manuscript.

Yep.

If ever there was a time-sucking, brain-snarfing monster, it's social media.

As I curled up on the couch during our spiritual retreat and stared at that striking year-end-review question, "Where is there clutter in my life?" I decided to go for bald honesty.

"Everywhere," I wrote, in pen.
And then, "Facebook."

•••••

The beauty of that year-end review was not the discussion
with Tom, although that was hugely important. The beauty was
in the intentional reflection, which I, by nature, love. It was also
in the intentional goal setting, which I, by nature, loathe. That's
where it got real for me: the blow-by-blow saying out loud what
I will do to eliminate the emotional and mental clutter. And for
me, it was one small thing: detach from social media—followed
by several important steps. Turn off all notifications. No more
surfing my newsfeed every three minutes. Check messages once
in the morning and once in the afternoon. And now, instead of
closing all my screens at 10:00 p.m., it would be 9:00 p.m. No
social media on whatever day I've identified as the best for Sabbath (this often shifts from week to week). And tell Erin, Dave,
and Tom what I'm doing.

So that's it, my one small practice for this month—which I'm
attempting, and failing, and attempting again to stretch into
the whole year. It may seem silly and, well, small. But it's prov-
ing to be ridiculously hard. On one level, it goes against every
professional-writer instinct I have; I'm hardwired to maintain
my public "platform"—as if I'm some kind of international
celebrity whose sales rankings will evaporate if I don't tweet
right now, this second, about the doughnut I'm currently de-
vouring. This is to say nothing of the grandparents who would
appreciate hourly documentation of their grandsons' escapades
(sample post: "Micah to me: 'I think I'm ready for bed. You
must be exhausted'").

Yet when I manage to follow the simple practice of detaching
from an anxious culture, I'm able to do that North Woods–retreat
inhale/exhale thing. I find time slowing down, my shoulders un-
clenching. Instead of waking up and immediately checking mes-

sages on my phone, I lie in bed for a while, letting the words of Psalm 90 remind me where I truly dwell: not online, not in 140 characters that will be here one second and gone the next, but in the Eternal One:

> Lord, you have been our dwelling place,
>   in all generations.
> Before the mountains were brought forth,
>   or ever you had formed the earth and the world,
>   from everlasting to everlasting, you are God.
> (Ps. 90:1–2)

Instead of focusing on a ravenous world that pretends to need me, I do something to prove I am not, in fact, God. Something that is not necessary for my children's survival. Something that doesn't give me the nagging feeling that I'm missing out. Instead of mindlessly surfing my newsfeed after putting the boys to bed—as if this counts as "maintaining my platform"—I purposefully stand in front of a bookshelf and think, "Hmm, what novel should I read now?" Time stretches. It spreads out before me like a down comforter. A leisurely hour before 10:00 p.m. prayer with Tom, just for reading? Yes, please. With the side bonus that my other commitments, including the five new spiritual practices I've started in as many months, don't seem so overwhelming. Funny how it works that way.

Erin's Story

My children sense the Sabbath like a dog senses an oncoming storm. Anxious that Mom might be attempting something other than answering their immediate needs for "snackies" and entertainment, they begin to howl: "I'm hungry. No, I want gum. Or maybe an apple. Candy! Can I have candy? Can I have some screen time? Can I have an apple? I meant a banana. With peanut butter. No, please don't peel it I said please don't peel it—no! You peeled it! Now it's ruined! What do you mean, I lost my screen time?"

Where was I? Ah yes, attempting Sabbath.

You know who's good at this? The guy who sleeps with his phone. Really.

Dave, the guy whose social media feed illuminates our bedroom ceiling well after I've pried myself from a novel and shut off the nightstand lamp. The guy who, starting in January, gave up social media one day a week, just like I did, and yet forgets (just like I do) for the ten minutes it takes his coffeemaker to percolate, every single time.

So he forgets sometimes. But otherwise he's good at this Sabbath thing.

The same month that we began our weekly social media fast, while visiting family in Ohio, Dave beckoned me out to his dad's shed with a text message: "Need you outside." I left his mom at their kitchen table to join Dave and his dad in the shed, where Dave was sorting long planks of oak from an old stable. Nail-and-bug-free oak to the right; too-knotty oak to the left. "Nail's sticking out right there. Watch it," my father-in-law warned, grabbing a board Dave handed to him.

"What's this for?" My jaw chattered in the January cold.

"I'm going to build a table," Dave replied over his shoulder.

"Like, for us?"

He grinned, an old brown wool hat pressing a pencil to his temple. "Yeah. I'll make it in the basement."

"Will the smell of horse manure go away?"

Ed and Dave chuckled. "Well, we hope." They carried as much wood to the van as I (in all my vast, no-carpentry experience) said was probably enough to build a table large enough for us and then more people. We loaded the girls and the dog, thanked Ed for the free lumber, and headed north (to the nearest gas station, where I made Dave buy enough pine-tree-shaped air fresheners to mask the stench).

All that winter Dave tromped downstairs on Sunday afternoons
to that pile of oak. He'd play Wilco and Pearl Jam albums, or
David Crowder; he'd sing along horribly and drink too much coffee. Sawdust caught in his eyebrows and wood chips on the belly
of his sweatshirt. The man was happy working with his hands. He
smiled a lot; he watched a lot of videos online about how to make
warped wood square. Sunday afternoon by Sunday afternoon, as
the winter melted into second winter into gray spring, his social
media notifications blinked, unanswered, while the table took a
rectangular shape, then grew legs. The legs were painted yellow
and the top was attached with bolts larger than I'd known existed.
It was finished.

We celebrated with a dinner party, some of my favorite people
on eight chairs around the table, candles flickering in mason jars.
I wiped up every spill, even the one that dripped between an invisible crack somewhere. (Hey, you try making six pieces of barn
wood seamless.)

It's beautiful, solid: our Sabbath table.

Dave's Sabbath table. Smelly wood turned means of grace for
our family. (And after the polyurethane finish, it didn't stink anymore, thankfully.) Dave got to be a creator, like his God. He did
this from a place of rest, like his God.

And now I fold a dozen loads of laundry on it each week. Just
this past Wednesday, Alice wrote a letter there to my cousin in
Africa, Louisa practiced her name on scrap paper with fat wash-
able markers, and I laid out stained but colorful cloth napkins,
straight from the laundry basket to the table's shiny walnut-
stained top.

Half a year later, Dave's moved on. He's making a bench from
wood that Sycamore Creek gave away when the church bought
and began remodeling an old building (more on that in chapter
8). The wood from the backs of disassembled pews leans against
Dave's workbench in the garage. He'll paint it turquoise, and I'll
sit on it to read Willa Cather and drink my chai.

Dave's Sabbath bench.

Who knew that the man who can't quit Twitter would leave very tangible reminders of his Sabbath rest around our house? Dave understood before I did that the Sabbath isn't a list of don'ts. It's freedom. We do this not just because God rested; we do it—resting and playing, not working—as an alternative to the "more bricks" mentality of the culture around us.[7] We don't check our work email on the Sabbath, because we're remembering that God has rescued us from slavery. Slavery to anything but God—"snackie" time and my children's whims and twelve radical practices included.

Which makes me wonder: If I rest, will my kids learn this rhythm? As I move beyond my practice of simply quitting social media for a day and into my own version of creative play, won't my children too? Isn't that what I want to teach them? Not the rules, but the freedom? What would it look like for Dave and me to take these things we're learning and practice all this as a family? Could we all take small steps together in this?

Back to Sarah

Some of you grasp this work/rest rhythm already. Thus, your challenge this month may be different. Others of you may realize, while reading this chapter, that you haven't set aside a day for Sabbath rest. Ever. Or that you need to detach from email or from channel surfing before bedtime. Or you may decide to complete a year-end review, and that's your one small thing when it comes to reflecting on your use or abuse of time (or time's abuse of you). Or maybe Tom's idea of a quarterly spiritual retreat strikes a chord; how might you build that into the coming year? Whatever it is, tell your community what you're up to. If need be, ask for help in making it happen, whether it's watching children, coordinating transportation, or subbing for you in the youth program one Sunday. At the very least, ask for prayer.

"So," Dave says to me at dinner, "does that mean when we see you on Facebook, we can post, 'Sarah, get off Facebook'?" "Yep," I say. And we laugh, but they know I'm serious.

~~~~ *Questions for Reflection and Discussion* ~~~~

1. Where is there emotional clutter in your life?
2. What keeps you from Sabbath rest? Who can hold you accountable?
3. What practical ways can you cut yourself off once a week from the 24/7 demands of communication technology? (Hide your phone, leave the house, etc.)
4. How might you talk about Sabbath rest with those in your life who don't want to participate?

~~~~ *For Further Reading* ~~~~

Brueggemann, Walter. *Sabbath as Resistance: Saying No to the Culture of Now*. Louisville: Westminster John Knox, 2014.

McKibben Dana, MaryAnn. *Sabbath in the Suburbs: A Family's Experiment with Holy Time*. St. Louis: Chalice Press, 2012.

Robinson, David. *The Busy Family's Guide to Spirituality: Practical Lessons for Modern Living from the Monastic Tradition*. New York: Crossroad, 2009.

7

VOWS

Date nights are cheaper than divorce.

—Tom Arthur

Joyful, lifelong fidelity will make our homes and marriages powerful signs of an attractive alternative to today's brokenness and agony.

—Ronald Sider[1]

Erin's Story

"So how's date night going?"

Crickets allegedly die off during winter, but I swear I heard some at the parsonage in February as Tom asked us about this month's practice: recovering date night.

Date night? Isn't this a little heavy on the "ordinary" part of "ordinary radical"? Yes and no. Christians hold no monopoly on date night, of course. But here's the radical part: when new monastics practice "supporting singles alongside monogamous married couples and their children," it's the word "alongside" that offers a glimpse of the kingdom. There's a lot to unpack in just one word.

"Alongside" should raise questions: How can we as a Christian body support one another in the vows we've taken in marriage or abstinence, the friendships we've created, the earthly relationships that are most important to us? How can we, the church, offer spaces of grace, hope, reconciliation, and even *fun* (hey, novelty!) not just for married couples but for the celibate? Widows? Singles? Single parents, the lonely, the heartbroken, the tired, the busy—all of us?

The answer is alarmingly simple in theory: we set aside time. Like the Sabbath, like prayer. Of course. Holy, set-apart time.

In theory, right?

Dave and I went on a date once, I think . . . back in October? Mom had the kids for the weekend, anyway. All that winter we were paying down debt, we had just survived feet upon feet of snow, and now in February Tom Arthur sat on his high horse and asked, "How's scheduling date night going?"

Crickets.

"That good, huh?"

Well, gee, Tom, do you know how expensive it is to hire a baby-sitter for three kids? How hard it is to find one? Do you know how hard it is to drive to Grandma in Ohio in February? Do you know how just, gosh, tired we are? Homeschooling, working, children's ministry, and no sidewalks on which to exercise away some stress? Tom, please. Christ, have mercy. *Cheeep, cheeep.*

Sadly, though, we had to admit that Tom was right. What sort of Christian witness does a joyless marriage offer to the world? What does it say about following Jesus if we're bending our schedules to the limit to feed the homeless, give rides to folks in our church family, lead small groups in intentional spiritual formation—and yet we don't talk to our spouses beyond saying, please, could you notice the blue light on the dishwasher once in a while? We must create a culture where we, Team Wasinger, celebrate each other as gifts from God, worth spending time and money on. The children, the dog, the bills, work, February, ministry, and family obligations—let alone the other practices and disciplines of faith—don't brake on their own to support these vows. We're not suddenly going to find ourselves alone together in the car, showered and dressed in something other than yoga pants, as it dawns on Dave that maybe we could make out now.

Neither does it appear, if you read enough books and articles written by the new wave of radical Christians, that being "on mission" with Jesus allows for such indulgences as getting dressed up and hiring a sitter once every so often. As Francis Chan asserts, a marriage should be practically effortless so long as each person is "on the battlefield" for Jesus. ("Honestly, we don't spend much time working on our unity. The unity has come as a result of the mission.") Really?

Please. *Please*—from the husband who spent an entire winter trying to pay off debt by working two jobs while his wife was snowed in with three young kids; from the couple who felt called to Michigan and lived apart for six months while they were in the process of a painfully awkward, financially devastating move—listen: dates matter. Holy, set-apart time matters. Yes, we find meaning and joy in fulfilling our Jesus-sized callings. Yes, marriage comes second after relationships with Christ. But these deep, intimate relationships are training grounds for sanctification, fun, and grace—if only we as a church put brackets around that holy time.

Speaking specifically to married couples, we have to park the crazy train. And then disembark. Standing there together, away from the fray, looking at each other as people, we get a clearer picture of who we are and where God's taking us. We listen. We engage. We imagine. We hope this counts as one of those moments when "the closer you listen, the more understanding you will be given" (Mark 4:24 NLT), because on that crazy train of adulting,

working, ministering, neighboring, and all the rest, it's difficult to
see whether we're growing at all into the character of Christ—or
just into busier versions of ourselves.

"Alongside" implies that we as a body are, again, part of a school
for conversion: we together value deep friendships and meaningful
marriages, and thus we together hold each other accountable to
promises we've made. This is radical in a culture that values sex
but not forever-and-ever, laundry-on-Tuesdays-and-Thursdays
monogamous relationships—or even (cue the reality-TV cameras)
elective celibacy. It's also radical among radical Christians who can,
however well intentioned, turn the mission into the main thing.
Jesus is the main thing. His relational approach should remind us
that though he often went out preaching, healing, and teaching,
he also withdrew with his closest friends. We should emulate that
rhythm if it's truly Jesus we're trying to follow.

Putting it simply: we made some promises—to ourselves, in
our communities, and with our church—to live as disciples of
Christ. How is what we're doing different from what the majority
culture is doing if these relationships aren't helping us form into
the character of Jesus? And how will these relationships form
our discipleship if we aren't working on them, making time for
them—and if our churches and communities aren't supporting us
through prayer, by listening, by making sure time apart happens,
and by lending a hand to those of us with kids at home?

Team Wasinger aimed for just a few more dates a year. If two
were our average, six would be phenomenal. If six were possible,
eight would blow it out of the water. And a dozen? A windfall.

The answer lay not in hiring babysitters (which we couldn't
afford anyway) but in our church family. "I'm intrigued by a babysitting swap," my friend Jana said after I'd pitched it to her. "Let's
do it." Jana gets the short end of the deal: we have three kids; she
and her husband, Mark, have two. She's one of those kind souls
who is energized by small children (Saint Jana, you can call her),
so she promises when my kids tackle her at the door, it's "so, so

good." "Miss Jana! Miss Jana! Watch how I can somersault!" "Miss Jana! I drew you a picture!" "Miss Jana! I lost a tooth!"

As Jana stands tall above the three jumping girls, we wave and head out.

"We'll be back before midnight, maybe," we joke.

"Take your time!" she says.

"See you next December then!"

We close the door behind us and we're free. We're free, and it's not costing us a cent.

This isn't rocket science—I'd bet parents were negotiating baby-sitting swaps back in the caves. But this "I'll watch your kids one weekend, and you can watch my kids the next" deal is what makes time apart possible—especially when Grandma is a three-hour drive away.

Besides saving us some cash on babysitters, the swaps help us connect with our spouses. Yup, that's pretty simple. More subtly, though, they reinforce other relationships within our church. Within the framework of covenantal friendships—deeply rooted in Sycamore Creek, practiced at the same time that we're doing the other life-of-faith stuff—this simple babysitting swap holds us as individuals accountable for what goes on in the private world of a marriage. "You guys haven't had a date night in a while," Jana says in one of her truth-telling texts. "Let's get that on the calendar. Remember, you chose each other. You didn't choose those kids." I do the same for her and Mark.

And when things turn tumultuous in a marriage (and they have, they do, and they will again), I have a few safe people with whom I can relax my shoulders, take off the smile, and say, "I just don't know. I just don't know." And they'll pray for me and tell me it's okay not to have it all figured out. These people remind me that God knows the end of the story. Somehow, we're stitched closer together, Dave and I, through these friendships that respect our marriage (as I respect their relationships). In time, I'll rub the shoulders of these same women and let them snot on my handkerchiefs. "It's fine. I just toss them right into the washer. That cotton can take it. Lady, it's hard, I know. Jesus knows."

It's messy, and saying we as a faith community "support" singles and marrieds-with-kids and everyone in between gets super delicate sometimes. We want it to be as simple as preaching about sex or marriage once every couple of years, or maybe just offering a small group for singles or newlyweds, parents or empty nesters. Our "support" must inch deeper if we want to be a subtle but powerful witness to a life with Christ, in community with a diverse and dynamic group. This means, as we build these friendships, we commit to open, hard, celebratory-and-lamenting accountability with folks.

Maybe the word "support" doesn't adequately convey the work we're doing here—we're not delicate tulips growing vulnerably in a pot. We're in a muddy garden, growing in clumps. We knot our roots together to protect each other from washing away in a downpour.

We're holding each other in place and holding each other upward, toward the sun, the Son.

Sarah's Story

Erin and Dave often accuse us of having it easy: Tabitha babysits our boys every Friday night. Yes, *every* Friday night. This is not a requirement; it's her gift. We could never afford to pay her what she's worth. But in Tabitha's mind, this is family. This is what you do. This is where the practice of hospitality pushes beyond mere living arrangements into something beautiful: a little vision of the church as family, these people as my people, made possible only in and through Christ. And meanwhile, to state the bald facts, as long as our marriage is healthy, Tabitha has a home. If our marriage falls apart from all this relentless do-gooding, where would she live? So, date night.

But we haven't always gone out every Friday. When we were first married, it was just us; dates seemed extra special, even a bit unnecessary. We had plenty of time alone (sometimes too much). So we scheduled dates randomly, and they were often a big deal: fancy dinners, dressing up, weekends at bed-and-breakfasts, lots of creative ways to dispose of our two-income excess. Then came graduate school, followed quickly by Isaiah House. Suddenly, not only did we have no disposable income, but because three meals a day took place in communal space, we found ourselves going for weeks without a private conversation.

It didn't take Tom long to declare this unacceptable.

"We're going out this Friday," he announced to our housemates, "so we won't be here for dinner. Actually, we won't be here on Friday nights, ever."

"But we love you guys!" I added.

Now, on one level, this weekly commitment felt totally selfish. We were abandoning our community—which included unhappily single men and women—to do something that seemed superfluous, something that felt like privilege and independent wealth and first-world excess. Granted, our budget was only ten dollars per week, enough for a foot-long sandwich and two teeny gelatos from the Tobacco District downtown. But it was the *idea* of date night.

"You're wearing a skirt!" the resident three-year-old guest exclaimed on one of those first Fridays as we headed for the door.

"I wish someone would take *me* out," said his young single mom, her newborn in her arms.

I paused awkwardly by the door.

She smiled. "But it's good for my son to see this. He needs to know that a good man treats his woman right."

I exhaled. "Thank you," I managed to say.

It was this brief, grace-filled exchange that showed us how, on a deeper level, our weekly date could be a way of strengthening, not abandoning, our community. When new monastics practice "support for celibate singles alongside monogamous married couples and their children," it's not only a way of saying that singles hold the same intrinsic worth as couples and families; it's affirming that relational vows are not incidental to the overall health of the community. When the boundaries of marriage are valued and upheld, the community is stronger. When the practices of celibacy in singleness (whether the person wishes to be single or not) are valued and upheld, it's a reminder that none of us is ultimately defined by his or her sexuality, nor is the nuclear family the apex of the Christian life.

A few weeks after that awkward escape from Isaiah House, Tom took that mom and her boys on a fun outing. We also watched David and Rebecca's boys on those rare times when they allowed themselves the luxury of going out. The support structures ran deep in all directions.

•••••

As my colleague Tim Otto reminds us, Jesus was not particularly interested in the American version of "family values." Sure, Jesus showed respect and even love for family. But what is startling, Tim writes, "is how often Jesus speaks against and disrupts family."[3] Not only was Jesus a celibate single, but on more than one occasion he dismissed the ties of blood altogether, claiming the fellowship of believers to be the true family of God (see Matt. 12:46–50). As Tim puts it, Jesus "revolutionized family by defining it as those who do God's will."[4]

In the community of Christ's body, therefore, we have the chance to dethrone the idol of the "perfect" nuclear family, which in Christ is eclipsed by an entirely different vision of fellowship in the kingdom of God. We have the chance to model for our sons that yes, a "good man" treats his significant other well, but a good man also treats the single woman, the single man, as his sister and brother in Christ. Their well-being matters. A good woman doesn't prize having a spouse above everything else, but instead sees herself upheld in a community that both honors her sexuality and values her gifts and strengths.

"When I come home," Tabitha tells me often, "this is sanctuary." She is a beautiful single woman, something that doesn't go

unnoticed out in the world. Recently she was propositioned by
the mechanic who worked on her van: her services in exchange for
his. When she told me this, I was so enraged I could barely speak.
"Did you report him? Did you call the Better Business Bureau?"
I sputtered. "No," she said. "I told him he had crossed the line.
And then I came home. To sanctuary."

In the home that Tom and I provide for this sister in Christ, she
makes our sons something yummy for dinner every Friday night.
They play games; they build elaborate forts out of blankets and
furniture; they eat way too much sugar, and she puts them to bed
buzzing with excitement. So the real win here, during this month
of February, is not really Tom's and mine at all: it's our entire
household's. Tabitha has a warm bed to sleep in after she tucks our
children in—a bed that is not threatened by a world that assumes
her singleness is there for the overtaking. When she's struggling in
her relationships, she takes me aside and says, "Please pray"—and
we do, right there. And meanwhile, she makes our weekly dates
possible by saying, in essence, "Remember those vows you made
to each other? You made them to the rest of us too. And I'm going
to hold you to them. Now get out of here."

So this has been our weekly practice for years, which means that
Tom and I had a hard time identifying what our unique practice
for relational vows would be during this year of small things. It
seemed miraculous that somehow we still managed date nights
week after week. Our budget is no longer just ten dollars: we've set
twenty-five dollars per week as our goal during the warmer months
and recently upped it to thirty-five dollars in the winters—because
picnics aren't an option in February. In fact, the biggest challenge
right now, we realized, is not the quantity of time—we manage
to pull this off almost every week—but the *quality* of the time.

This includes not only the dinner-and-movie part of date night
but the sex too. As Tom will be the first to tell you, it's not particularly inspiring to "renew your vows" next to the world's most
unsexy object, the baby monitor. Making out with one hand on

the door to keep it closed is not anyone's favorite emotional high. Even while we were at Isaiah House, without children of our own, we engaged in elaborate door locking and subterfuges. Babies or no babies, attempting to keep your sex life intact while living in community is not particularly sexy.

So for this month focused on vows, we eventually determined that on those vacations when we stay with our various parents, we would take that opportunity to get away for an entire night, just the two of us. Which required some shifting to our budget (scaling down the cost of weekly dates sometimes, pulling funds from elsewhere) and planning ahead, but the results have been worth it: the extended time together—and, Tom would add, the sex.

Seems like a small thing, a night away. But, as Erin said, sometimes the whole community must put a bracket around the vows we've made and tell us, "We've got this. Get out of here."

Back to Erin

This is what it felt like when, at nine years of marriage, I realized I was supported in community: cold nose, heart beating wildly, burning eyes closed, my head lifted slightly upward, Dave's warm hand resting in mine as Rachmaninoff's notes inside the dark theater took flight from sheet music to strings and horns.

This is a radical date night for this married mom of three. Can you see it? So many notes the Composer orchestrated to make this possible: The free tickets from a friend who plays viola at Sycamore Creek and had lugged her instrument to small group every Thursday for eight weeks this winter. Jana at home with my three girls, reading with them before bedtime. Tom and Sarah asking us week after week, "How is date night going?" I realized I trusted the Composer, God, more because I was only just beginning to hear the complexity of the orchestration in my marriage.

I saw us supported, loved, regardless of our pasts, which aren't the kind of snowy-white church stories of our friends' lives. This is a story of redemption—which happened to be Sergei Rachmaninoff's game too. The Russian composer's first work had been an utter failure, and he soon spiraled into a deep depression.[5] It was only quietly that he began working on the second piece, which Dave and I heard that night in Lansing. Music awakens the bucolic daydreamer in me. I understand it as I understand math (remember, *I cannot*), yet I recognized the redemption in this second piece, this romantic, evocative Symphony no. 2. Familiar to me as the story of how Dave and I met (college newspaper), familiar to me as my own disreputable relational past and our dicey first few years of marriage—I recognized God making something beautiful where we wouldn't have predicted. The Creator wove us into relationship with himself, with church, with others.

Yes. I held Dave's hand on his knee, squeezed. A Russian composer wrote my marriage's theme a hundred years before Dave and I were wed (as Russian composers do).

•••••

We need this, these holy times of setting ourselves apart from the fray. The support we receive from our community gives us permission to take a new perspective, to lighten up, to laugh. The time apart isn't a luxury or a distraction from God's "mission" for marriage or singleness. Fun is part of the mission: laugh so others can hear you; testify to the life-giving relationships God has drawn you to, both within the covenant of marriage and with others in community.

So what about you?

If you're married, do you have a trusted friend who holds your marriage in high esteem (especially when you don't)? If you're single, do you have someone who sees you not as the Missing Piece but instead as completely beloved by God and your community? Do you have someone who understands how you feel about being single or married, divorced or widowed? Have you shared with anyone your hopes, your longings? Could you be so vulnerable? Because in being this boldly honest, we're moving beyond "support" as a euphemism for benign interest and into physically feeling the weight of burdens and the weightlessness of one another's joys—truly supporting one another.

Where to begin? Well, look around at your church family. Are there people who've been married awhile who can share dinner with you and your spouse once a month? If you've celebrated quite a few anniversaries, are there engaged couples you could have over for brunch after worship? What about coffee with just guys or just gals one Sunday afternoon, then again in a month or two?

Get to know each other and the vows you've taken in marriage or singleness: that's the first step. Hold each other's vows as worth fighting for. Resist the urge to fix—instead, pray. Be there. Be in touch. Be transparent. This is how we prepare the soil for friendships; this is the work of growing together in vulnerable accountability. When the storms come—be it money problems, temptations, or any other—our roots will be so tangled up we just might hold firm.

~~~~~ *Questions for Reflection and Discussion* ~~~~~

1. Have you named aloud to your covenantal friends the vows you've taken in marriage or singleness? Does sharing details with a trusted friend about your deepest, most intimate relationships come naturally? What model do you have for doing this?

2. What practices would help you feel more supported within your community? How can your community fight for the relational vows you've taken?

3. Who in your church needs support in his or her relationships? How might you provide some of that support?

4. Ask a friend each time you meet: What are you celebrating in your personal life right now? Where are you struggling? How can I pray for you?

For Further Reading

Miles, Carrie A. *The Redemption of Love: Rescuing Marriage and Sexuality from the Economics of a Fallen World.* Grand Rapids: Brazos, 2006.

Rische, Stephanie. *I Was Blind (Dating) but Now I See: My Misadventures in Dating, Waiting, and Stumbling into Love.* Carol Stream, IL: Tyndale, 2016.

Roberts, Ted, and Diane Roberts. *Sexy Christians: The Purpose, Power, and Passion of Biblical Intimacy.* Grand Rapids: Baker Books, 2011.

Thomas, Gary. *Devotions for a Sacred Marriage.* Grand Rapids: Zondervan, 2005.

———. *Sacred Marriage: What If God Designed Marriage to Make Us Holy More Than to Make Us Happy?* 2002. Reprint, Grand Rapids: Zondervan, 2015.

Winner, Lauren. *Real Sex: The Naked Truth about Chastity.* Annotated ed. Grand Rapids: Brazos, 2006.

8

planted in the church

In essence, the parish is a dare to your faith.

—*The New Parish*[1]

Sarah's Story

"Sycamore Creek Church . . . ," mused the woman I chatted with at the checkout one slushy March day. "Weren't y'all pumping gas at the Marathon on Mt. Hope Avenue a few weeks ago? You're the church next door to the gas station."

"You remember that?" I said, astonished.

Okay, so evangelism isn't my top spiritual gift. But keep in mind: for fifteen years SCC had been difficult to find, hidden away in a Christian school in a suburban office park. Describing our location to prospective guests took some explaining, and many of them never showed up. (Erin and Dave were an exception, and even they got lost on their first visit.) Other than our Church-in-a-Diner on

Monday nights, missionally we seemed to have no obvious focus; we sometimes wondered whether, if we ceased to exist, anyone outside our church would notice. But when, right before Christmas, we had moved from suburbia into an old unoccupied urban church building surrounded by residential streets, suddenly we registered on the map.

"Oh yes, I remember," the woman said. "It was freezing. I couldn't believe y'all were out there. But I pulled in and got free gas."

"Well," I stammered, "we'd love to see you on Easter. Sunday services are at 9:30 and 11. You can come as you are."

"I'll do that," she said with a firm nod.

A few weeks before this conversation, members of our church had taken over the local Marathon gas station (with the owner's permission) in single-digit temperatures, offering to pump gas so folks didn't have to exit their cars—and contributing five dollars toward their purchase. It was Ash Wednesday, prime time for letting the community know we're there for them. Meanwhile, the station owner's name is Ash. (C'mon! You can't make this stuff up.)

SCC had become visible as the neighborhood church on the block, smack within Lansing's city limits. But my mind hadn't quite made the shift. SCC was a suburban church; this was a key part of the narrative, right? It was the essential ingredient of the divine joke I kept telling. Isn't it just like God—har, har—to send someone who had purposefully lived in the inner city to suburbia instead? That was the script. This year of small things was supposed to be an uphill battle, a few families blazing a trail of radical faith that no one else had considered before.

After all, many of us are drawn to new monasticism because, let's be honest, our local churches can seem a little tame, if not downright disappointing. We'd like to see our congregations take bold action for the sake of the poor, the struggling. Not just, say, occasionally giving money to an agency that's trying to stop world hunger, but each family in the congregation having someone over for Easter dinner who doesn't look/talk/smell like us.

Not just occasionally collecting supplies for school backpacks, but the entire congregation partnering with a struggling local school to build mentoring relationships and support teachers. Big things. And when our churches fail to do those big things, we're tempted to wonder if we're in the right church—indeed, if *any* church as a monolithic institution is the right church—or if we should jump ship.

That's when the communities of new monasticism begin to glow with a kind of holy, prophetic allure: at least *they* are doing big things for "the least of these," right? Not that new monastic communities intend themselves to be a substitution for the local church—new monastics are quick to tell you this, which is why "humble submission to Christ's body, the church," is among their twelve marks—but it's tempting to approach new monasticism that way. Halfway through this year of small things, I was still wrestling with that temptation.

But now, as if to defy the script, my own church had done a big thing. It had made a huge move that trumped all my individual attempts at small things. That's because it involved an entire congregation, not just a few overeager individuals. In fact, roughly 50 percent of our members and regular attenders, at that point in SCC's history, already resided, not in suburbia, but in south Lansing, within minutes of our new building. On the first Sunday that we worshiped there, several of them walked to church.

This wasn't quite the first mark of new monasticism, "relocation to abandoned places of Empire"—our church's nearest neighborhoods are family friendly and walkable, close to celebrated river trails and the city zoo—but for the suburbanites in our congregation, it was close. Lansing's crime rates tend to be higher than the national average; 2013 data from the FBI identify it as one of America's top ten most dangerous cities with populations under two hundred thousand.[2] So this move was, to quote the authors of *The New Parish*, a kind of dare.[3] Dare you claim this family of faith, for better or worse? Dare you submit to this body, even when it veers from the script? Dare you let it shape your identity, your lifestyle, even your sense of place?

So in this month of March I had some soul-searching to do, some rescripting of what had become a key narrative. What if I had been wrong about this whole church thing? Yes, the bishop had appointed us, and in some ways the appointment system can seem to take away your sense of agency, the assertion that you can in fact *choose* to bind yourself in covenant to a people. But I was already bound to these people in baptism; I was daily choosing this body, even as this body, in Christ, had already chosen me. And meanwhile I chose to walk with Tom as he chose to submit himself to ecclesial authority. So there was plenty of choosing. What I hadn't yet chosen was a willingness to let my church—not just me or my family alone—participate in the change I was praying for in the world.

I mean, if my congregation could surprise me by taking a step of radical faith in regard to its location, a step that to many might seem unwisely downwardly mobile, what else could it do? What else were members of my congregation *already doing* that I had chosen—yes, chosen—to overlook or dismiss? What if a step of faith for one person or family in the local church is a step of faith for everybody? Even more importantly, what if my job isn't to be some kind of spiritual superhero, firing on all new monastic cylinders, but to pay attention to what folks in my own church are already doing and then offer support?

The parsonage was still in suburbia. For the foreseeable future, Tom and I would fail at relocating to an "abandoned place of Empire." But because we had bound ourselves to this local body, this innovative church, we were also bound to two people and their daughters, who were ready to go where God was leading.

Erin's Story

Depression was a forty-pound cat sleeping on my shoulders that March as I watched the cars kick up snow on the country road outside our rental. I tried to articulate or to pray away the sensation that I was coveting something I couldn't have—namely, a home of our own, in a place that would feel connected, warm, and more permanent. Meanwhile, Dave was beginning to wonder, was this it, this piecemeal existence on the outskirts of a city with a self-esteem problem? The late snow and omnipresent grayness of early spring can fuel all sorts of existential crises.

Memories flooded back of running in the dawn light over Oshkosh's Wisconsin Street bridge; of strolls with the dog and the girls on sidewalks, to parks, to friends' houses. And the longer I'd been away from Oshkosh, the rosier the memories had become. No city was as Midwestern. No church was as authentic as Water City had been. There'd been small group and potlucks and holidays spent together. No place was as Oshkosh as Oshkosh. Yet I knew we couldn't go back. For one, we'd burned through savings and took on more debt just to *get* to Michigan—we were the settlers who used the wood from their Conestoga wagons to build their cabins; the wheels were fuel. We were mimicking Abraham, called to a land outside our own imaginations, camping in the wilderness with our children as heirs to this strange adventure, and Abraham didn't go back. We grumbled, not wanting to believe this was the promised land, afraid to drink from the stream of relationships around us in case we would soon leave the Midwest too. In Michigan, we had adopted the next-door neighbors as grandparents; we'd joined as partners in Sycamore Creek's mission. We had friends, and I could even drive across town without accidentally getting on the eastbound ramp when I was westbound. Yet my depression-cat would hiss, "It won't be long before you have to uproot again and start all over."

Yet—and this is a big yet—Sycamore Creek Church was settling into its new neighborhood; we as a congregation joined the work that God was already doing in Lansing. Already growing in the same spot were neighbors, schools, nonprofits, businesses, and other places of worship. As we acclimated ourselves to our new surroundings, we intentionally bumped into those who lived, worked, learned, and passed through our neighborhood. Our branches became entangled as our staff took "field trips" to meet with those who had longer legacies in Lansing. We began to dream about joining their work, and some of our neighbors were compelled to come to worship to share what they're passionate about and what our neighborhood needs. All this grafting, all this connecting ourselves to these others, is critical to our own growth.

Don't miss that illustration: picture a tree—or is it two trees?— growing as conjoined twins in a woods, limbs entangled and connected, beautifully inseparable thanks to years of steady growth in close proximity to each other. You might wonder, how did that happen? Is that one tree—or two? Which tree came first? What would happen if one of them died? You might marvel at the work of time and proximity in nature. Otherwise minor, insignificant, but repetitive rubbing of protective bark—imagine branches scraping together in the wind—exposes the trees' inner layers to each other. Over time, cells multiply where branches touch; they grow together, most without human intervention. God, in this case, is the great Horticulturist, creating shared life from what was simply shared proximity.

Following that logic then, when Sycamore Creek Church moved into the neighborhood as a congregation, the wind started up. We're being grafted. Growing between us and the neighborhood are relationships that will, we pray, be so integral to the places we touch as a congregation that people might start to wonder: Is that one place or two? Sycamore Creek—church or neighborhood?[4] How did they even grow like that? What would happen if one died? What happens when one thrives?

The winds stirred up new dreams for us as a family that March. "What if *we* stayed too?" I asked Dave one night. "What if this is our church and Lansing is our city? What if we get the kids in school" (more on that in the next chapter) "and start really living like we're going to stay?" And apparently God slapped hands together and said "magic word," because obstacles fell. First, the money thing: we had no down payment (we'd used the Conestoga wheels for fuel, remember). Then a friend pointed us to down-payment grants from the city and state. We had a lease, yet when we asked, our landlord said we could cancel it at any time, no penalty. We had to figure out a million details (a dining room large enough for the Sabbath table, sidewalks for walkability, school enrollment), but with waiting and prayer, we—

Wait. I shouldn't gloss over those moody March, April, and May days, those long afternoons when we had no idea where the kids would go to school, where we'd live, whether we were crazy, and whether we really, really wanted to do this. Three months doesn't sound like a long time, but in those excruciatingly boring afternoon hours were doubts, crouched and waiting to lure us elsewhere. Warning: if you're going to bring someone's grand-children to a place where the schools aren't ranked top in the state and where police sirens wail at all hours—where the majority of new businesses are medical marijuana shops—you're going to have doubts. When disagreements cause people you love and with whom you've worshiped to start "church shopping," you're going to question whether it's insane or merely misguided to graft yourself to anyone else, let alone a whole body of people you don't have a lot in common with except Jesus.

Dave especially did his share of reckoning with what it means to practice stability. Dave is the guy who wanted to document humanity from a war zone, or at least live in a big urban area; he thought we'd stay in Lansing two or three years before mov-ing to a bigger metro daily. He loves telling visual stories at the *Lansing State Journal*, but it takes more creativity to see how you're documenting humanity in a sluggish capital city. Some days you're shooting a Big Ten football game, and some days you're shooting a ground-breaking ceremony at Goodwill. Some days it's race relations conferences; some days it's taxidermied chip-munks reenacting a football game (this happened—bonus photo at www.yearofsmallthings.com). Do you see? *We understand how hard it is to be tethered. We know how shiny the Emerald City looks from a distance.* The dream of stability and the desire to graft oneself onto a church doesn't come on a person all at once, at least not in our case. There were months of tedious, emotional, and gut-checking conversations and prayer—lots of prayer, late at night, staring at the ceiling, not even talking. We understand.

We're no longer in the realm of small things. And who saw this coming? We were the couple who ruined Christmas, wanted a trophy for giving up social media on Sundays, and couldn't find time to date.

Yet.

Amid the doubts and failures, where we assented to be grafted, God began the miracle of new growth. Easter stuff.

Which brings us to the apex of the Christian calendar. This year, Easter was early April. For some (maybe misguided) reason, Tom invited the congregation to ceremonially make holes in the walls of our church's new-old building, to mark us doing something new: beginning renovations on what would become the Connection Café, a local spot for free coffee and Wi-Fi. Our church's neighborhood lacks a "third space," a place to meet or relax. So, rather than first tackling the sanctuary (complete with traditional church-red carpet) or the media system, we chose to remodel the main floor as a way to tell our neighbors, "Come on in." Tom, I'm sure, made some allusion to Christ breaking out of the tomb, but all we heard was "make holes in the wall," and he didn't have to ask twice. Drywall went flying; people smiled at each other through the newly revealed gaps between studs.

Isaiah 43 came to mind: "I am about to do something new. See, I have already begun! Do you not see it?" (v. 19 NLT). The energy was palpable.

And then . . . it was time to go home. Dave and I gathered our three girls as people returned hammers and crowbars to the toolbox. The din quieted to conversation, and we walked across the parking

lot to our van, alone. We drove south on Pennsylvania Avenue, past
neighborhoods, a hospital, car dealers, and big-box stores, past
the city limits and then the next township's line too. We drove by
farm fields not yet thawed and woods not yet budded. We pulled
into our driveway—twenty-some minutes after we'd left our urban
church—in anticlimactic silence, our Easter alleluia a faint echo,
a dim memory. Drywall dust wasn't even left on my hands. Our
people were in Lansing, and we needed to be too. That's all. We
needed to be with our church.

Insert several more weeks of sighing, listening to too much
Sufjan Stevens, and staring into the middle distance.

Then came May, another Sunday after church. We turned our
van onto a quiet residential street just south of Sycamore Creek's
neighborhood. Technicolor green leaves above our heads gave the
street a surreal aura, but when we pulled up in front of the Cape
Cod with the for-sale sign in the yard, we braked hard.

"Dave."

"I'll grab a flyer."

"Are we going to see this house on the inside?" The five-year-
old was practically bursting from her seat at the chance to run
through yet another empty house while Mom and Dad looked
the other way.

"Dave, I have a feeling about this one." I took in the details on
the flyer, now in my hands: a kitchen large enough for the Sabbath
table, a partially finished basement. Goosebumps on my arms . . .

An hour later, we were taking selfies in the bathroom mirror,
red shag carpet under our feet and velvety wallpaper behind us.

Two hours later, we were making an offer.

Two days later, it was ours.

Watch—watch what God does with your small things.

Now, our southside neighborhood isn't where you'd expect to
find textbook new monastics, whoever those are. People mow their
lawns here; no overt drug activity keeps us up at night. The Cape
Cods and small ranch facades repeat in slight variations of white,

beige, green. But it is a mixed neighborhood in terms of age, race, and income. We're not in some idyllic or isolated spot. Our house is just north of a medical marijuana dispensary and a run-down carryout place whose paint announces its wares: liquor, beer, used tires. The neighborhood elementary school looks tired somehow.

Lansing might not fully fit the description "abandoned place of Empire," but it is certainly a struggling, under-resourced urban center.[5] We pass strip malls, strip clubs, and stretches of dilapidated homes on the way to the library or the grocery store. The reputation of the midsized Midwestern city's schools mimics that of many urban districts (more on that in chapter 9).[6] We knew all this (we're journalists; research is our hobby), so it wasn't romanticism that made us choose Lansing. It began with a lament. It angled toward a conclusion with church, when Tom asked a bunch of us to knock ceremonial holes in the wall. It ended—or rather began—with a little house on the south side.

That doesn't mean other suburbanites from Sycamore Creek Church are moving in droves to Lansing, although, as Sarah mentioned, a good half of our members lived in south Lansing already. And a number of neighbors near the church have begun attending—"they" are becoming "we," and "we" are becoming "they." But if we as a family are practicing stability—and if we know ourselves to be supported by prayers, relationships with the neighbors, and a shared love for the people around our new venue—then that's a win for the church. We as a family don't have to perfectly exhibit all twelve marks of new monasticism. But I think we grew into one this spring.

We've started to see our neighbors as branches that we might be grafted to as the wind may blow or the great Horticulturist works some magic. I'm not sure how knowing my neighbors' names and bringing them scones for Christmas does it, but grafting takes time. How are you sharing mundane moments with the people who live closest to you? This is not classic "missional" or "evangelistic" stuff. We don't lead with "Hey, have you met

Jesus?" It's much more subtle. We don't look alike or organize our lives around the same values, yet we still talk about our kids while we're raking leaves. By the dawn light, we yell at our dogs to stop chasing squirrels; we wave to each other in our pajamas from our respective side doors. We know their routines, and they know ours. We're starting to know people "in their ordinariness."[7] And someday, we may know them in their pain, their triumphs, and whatever else falls in the middle.

Back to Sarah

The overachieving part of me that heckled the Wasingers and their budget back in October with "Game on!" could easily throw in the towel right now. If this were merely about individual families attempting to make some radical changes to their daily Christian practices in order to more faithfully witness about Jesus, then the Wasingers would win, hands down. "Guys," I could whine, "this was supposed to be the year of *small* things, remember? Stop showing us up."

But if what I've learned about the body of Christ is true—that we're engrafted into this people and thus this neighborhood—then the Wasingers' "win" is everybody's win. Their prophetic witness to God's grace and presence in our local urban center is our witness; their struggles, too, will be ours. The potholes on South Pennsylvania Avenue, the medical marijuana shops, the struggling schools—those problems are now my problems, our problems, because they affect members of my church, my friends. This is a sad but honest truth about myopic human self-involvement. But the longer our church stays in its new neighborhood, the larger that pool of friends grows. So the question that will animate much of the rest of this book (particularly chapter 12) becomes, How can we as a worshiping community leverage our resources and our access to power, on behalf of those who struggle, to make for change in *God's* city?

In the meantime, we Arthurs are back to small things. Grocery envelopes. Prayer at 10:00 p.m. Scaling back on social media. Making sure Tabitha's bathroom has toilet paper.

It's Erin who is quick to remind me that hospitality is no small thing. "Dave and I are flunking at this, remember?" she said one Tuesday night as we shuffled Tabitha's placemat around to make room for five Wasingers. "It's been eight months. We still have no idea what to do about hospitality."

"Well, I've been thinking—" Tom began.

"Of course you have," I said.

"No, really," he continued, unperturbed. "There are actually a bunch of folks in our church who share their households with other people—with friends or parents or grown children or even the homeless. And most of them have expressed to me how hard it is. What if we got everyone together for dinner? You know, to connect and share ideas. So they don't feel so crazy."

"Hey!" Erin said. "Can I crash that party?"

This is where it starts: the looking up and around instead of navel-gazing our own spiritual quandaries. I'm a first-class navel-gazer: it is the curse of being a writer. To quote Stanley Hauerwas: "There is something about writing that seems to make us particularly unaware of our self-involvement."[8] But by the grace of covenantal friendship and by engraftedness into the people of God, I'm forced to stop whining and start paying attention. Where in my faith community are people doing the things I can't right now? And how can I lend them my support?

Which is how, on the last Sunday in March, we found ourselves with a dozen people from church sitting around the parsonage table. That table! The epicenter of so many conversations about following Jesus, so many slow conversions, including my own. That night at dinner we found ourselves in the company of retired folks, single women, young couples (some with children, some without), a range of God's people all practicing hospitality in their homes. We told our stories, our struggles, our biggest questions.

Yadiel, a Puerto Rican, explained how in his culture hospitality is totally normal; sleeping on couches while you get settled is just what you do. (What wasn't said: "You whites are just a little nuts about this single-family home thing.") Tom passed around copies of the hospitality covenant that we've used in our household (see appendix B). Erin listened quietly. We prayed.

Maybe I'm a slow study, but this seemed like a big thing. Here were a dozen people in our congregation who were not only looking for Jesus in the stranger but telling Jesus, "My home is yours." And if there were a dozen taking this particular step of faith, perhaps there were a dozen others living more simply so they could give more, or doing the hard work of racial reconciliation—or any number of radical Christian practices that I was trying to check off my list. If I was truly grafted into this body, then all my overachieving instincts needed to take a back seat. Instead of doing, I need to be listening, praying, and then supporting.

And perhaps that's you too. Perhaps you realize that you aren't nailing all twelve marks of new monasticism, but others in your church are nailing *some* of them. These folks may never have heard of "radical faith," but they've discerned a call to follow Jesus in ways our culture may view as really, really odd. Maybe your small thing this month is to simply hear their stories and then to follow up by offering support.

Or maybe you need to take it up to ten thousand feet: What local worshiping community are you planted in? Maybe your small thing begins with erasing the phrase "church shopping" from your vocabulary and committing to a place, even (or especially) if it doesn't live up to your wish list. What if instead of leaving a church without notice, you discerned with your covenantal friends for a long time? What if you chose these people anyway?

Or what if you shut down the search for a new job in a new place and just stayed put? Are you growing into a certain plot of earth, alongside a worshiping community and its neighbors? In what ways could you think about your neighborhood as a particular location where God has placed you, on purpose? Maybe the small thing for you is committing to know your church's neighborhood or your own neighbors (if they aren't the same people). Begin to see the space where you live as an extension of your local church: the place you become known to your neighbors and begin to know them too. And vice versa: Stop at the coffee shop near your church. Buy your groceries from the corner store across from where you worship. Take walks in that neighborhood. Participate in a community cleanup there. Pray.

As a church, what does it look like to seek common ground in the place where your church worships or lives? Who are your neighbors: close business owners, school communities, or neighborhood associations? Who is God already using—however subtly—as agents for peace and reconciliation right where you are?

When we are on the ground, literally, in our church's neighborhood, we can start to see the work already begun; our imaginations start kicking around how we might join. And over time, we may—we pray—start to see this *being there* as integral, inseparable to our conversion.

As Erin indicated, we can be grafted only if we're close enough to touch.

~~~~~ *Questions for Reflection and Discussion* ~~~~~

1. What does "humble submission to Christ's body, the church" look like for you?
2. When is leaving a worshiping community healthy—and when does it become idolatry for us to find a church that looks more "like us"?
3. How close are you to your church, physically and emotionally? In what ways does the distance or space impact your walk with God?

4. Which people in your congregation are practicing some of the marks of new monasticism (at least, that you know of)? In what ways can you connect with them to learn their stories and offer support?

~~~~~ *For Further Reading* ~~~~~~~~~~~~~~~~~~~~~

Jacobsen, Eric. *Sidewalks in the Kingdom: New Urbanism and the Christian Faith*. Grand Rapids: Brazos, 2003.

Otto, Tim, and Jon R. Stock. *Inhabiting the Church: Biblical Wisdom for a New Monasticism*. Eugene, OR: Cascade Books, 2007.

Smith, C. Christopher. *Slow Church: Cultivating Community in the Patient Way of Jesus*. Downers Grove, IL: InterVarsity, 2014.

Sparks, Paul, Tim Soerens, and Dwight J. Friesen. *The New Parish: How Neighborhood Churches Are Transforming Mission, Discipleship and Community*. Downers Grove, IL: InterVarsity, 2014.

Wilson-Hartgrove, Jonathan. *The Wisdom of Stability: Rooting Faith in a Mobile Culture*. Brewster, MA: Paraclete Press, 2010.

9

kid monasticism

The lump of clay, from the moment it comes under the transforming hand of the potter, is during each day and each hour of the process, just what the potter wants it to be at that hour or on that day, and therefore pleases him; but it is very far from being matured into the vessel he intends in the future to make it.

—Hannah Whitall Smith[1]

I worry that Jesus drinks himself to sleep when he hears me talk like this.

—Anne Lamott[2]

Erin's Story

We were wrapping up a lesson on subtraction, Alice and I, that April afternoon; then we read about British kings from long ago. A children's retelling of Shakespeare's *The Tempest* was the last play we diagrammed on the chalkboard. Check, check, check. In April we were ticking off boxes on a clipboard; our homeschooling days were numbered. As these long days at home together disappeared under our feet like an escalator step, though, our legs hovered, unsure where they'd land. We five Wasingers had vertigo as we tarried there in midair, our fingers clicking through online listings of homes all over south Lansing.

We knew we'd be moving closer to church soon, but at this point we didn't yet know where we'd land. We knew we'd no longer be homeschooling, but we didn't know which public schools our children would attend. Evaporated were the feel-good, small-things experiments, along with the last piles of ash-gray snowmelt. Now there were big puddles, big experiments. Our kids' boots were about to get really, really wet with decisions driven by God and their parents. Suddenly this year of small things was full of big things that would affect some very small people in some very big ways.

When you saw our children's names on the covenant at the beginning of this book, did you pause, asking what role these kids had in deciding if they would participate? Did you wonder what the consequences would be? We did too. It's one thing to share a weekly meal with friends, pray together, or put dimes and quarters into those "give-save-spend" jars. But moving?

When you add "with kids" to the end of the twelve new monastic marks, those practices begin to muddle together as impossibilities. Reconciliation among racial groups doesn't seem plausible when I can't keep three sisters from waging a 7:00 a.m. war over the bathroom. Or maybe you sense, like us, that relocating to an abandoned place of Empire becomes crazy complicated when children hit school age. At the end of the day, new monasticism still sounds like a great hobby for a single, child-free, debt-free young adult.

But here you are, and if you've read this far, chances are you believe (or are starting to think) that where you live, where you worship, or where your children learn dictates a lot about how you'll be spending your time and energy—and with whom you'll be in relationship. You may see Jesus beckoning you to join him elsewhere, and you may be ready to go, but you look down and there's a small child holding your hand. And it's not as simple as just dragging that child along.

As Dave and I read about new monasticism, we as parents had to ask ourselves questions. First, was there room for nuance? Was it possible to live out the values of new monasticism in some ways but not in others? Second, were we poseurs? Were we modeling for our children an à la carte faith? More difficult to answer: Were we—are we—committed to signing up our children for downward mobility for Christ? After all, by virtue of being in our family, they will share the risks and rewards. How much of the risk should they know? How much of the reward will they also grow to value? This new challenge went way beyond "Mom and Dad made us spend, like, two dollars on Christmas. I'm damaged for life." Much more was at stake.

Our experiment, then, this April was once again *discernment*. We had two choices: we could enroll the kids in a Lansing elementary school, since presumably we'd be living there by fall; or we could apply for a lottery of spots in a suburban district between our rural rental and south Lansing. One would allow us to be completely invested in whatever neighborhood we moved into; the other would put the girls in a system that, frankly, performs better. We were tempest-tossed with emotions from April until July.

We knew the facts. Like many urban centers, Lansing's schools are widely panned for low test scores, program cuts, and budget shortages that have led to the elimination of teacher jobs.[3] Elementary schools have lost art, music, and physical education instructors, leaving the burden on classroom teachers. Changing demographics, charter schools, and the state's Schools of Choice program have all drained enrollment. The proliferation of choices has swung demographics dramatically: twenty-five years ago, the district was 58 percent white, 42 percent nonwhite; it's now about

29 percent white, 71 percent nonwhite.[4] About 71 percent of students qualify for free or reduced-price lunches, a standard measure of poverty.[5]

Dave and I hate the segregation, but we also aren't fans of what goes on in the classrooms. Friends warned us about Lansing's burned-out teachers, an unclear curriculum plan, and few measurable indicators of improvement. While, on the one hand, this could sound like rich soil for developing our children's empathy and adaptability, Dave and I worried they would, in a chaotic environment, lose their love for learning. (And if kids are going to school to learn math and reading, and most kids in a given school fail math and reading, shouldn't we *all* be asking why?)

Yet my kids are school-aged *now*. Urgency undergirded our discussions.

Compounding our problem of discernment were two facts. First, in all the other experiments so far this year, we could invite other folks to join us or give us advice. A low budget for groceries? Game on, Arthurs! But in this case we knew no one who'd recently chosen Lansing schools, which spoke to our limited circle of friendship as newcomers and our mostly white, suburban social pool. So long as the Arthurs reside in the parsonage in Holt, Micah and Sam will attend one of the area's best elementary schools. Second, throughout this discernment process, Dave and I knew we would be opening ourselves up to misinterpretation. Our gung-ho radical friends might see us as hypocrites for embracing a city but abandoning its schools; our more cautious friends might think we were bleeding-heart liberals making a big deal out of an easy decision.

We prayed. We talked ad nauseam to friends far and wide.[6] We even contacted Tom and Sarah's former housemates at Isaiah House, David and Rebecca, who spoke to this conundrum: when their oldest son began kindergarten, they reviewed numerous options, eventually settling on a public magnet school. But it's not perfect. Some years they do extra work at home when a child is struggling. They remain open to other options if ever the boys aren't thriving.

In books that we read, new radicals and new monastics seemed to be entirely silent on this issue. Even a contemporary prophet like Ronald J. Sider gave us only one line in *Just Politics*: "Parents must have the freedom to choose schools that share their values."[7] Confusingly, though, an earlier chapter asserted that choosing to participate in evil systems is just as sinful as adultery.[8] The tension between the two statements could have filled an entire book. Because we cannot separate being parents from being followers of Christ, we can't blindly assume that the choices we make for our children's education don't have consequences for our local district, our city, and the broader society. Schools of Choice–type programs are hardly victimless. What do our choices mean for the underprivileged schools our kids don't attend? What are the schools losing beyond per-pupil grants from the state when families choose to enroll elsewhere?

In the end, here's what we learned: *no rules exist*, mercifully. Faithful Christians disagree about education, which points to the myriad ways God can move in the lives of our kids—not to mention our cities. In the end, it would come down to discerning what God was calling *our* family to do, in our particular context, within the loving and prayerful support of our covenantal friendships and congregation.

It came down to a lot of dinner conversations, with our kids listening in.

•••••

Picture the parsonage table again. Each week that we spent in the no-man's-land between quitting homeschooling and not knowing what came next, Dave and I unloaded on Tom and Sarah our latest research, friends' opinions, and conflicted emotions.

"The Lansing board of education cut the art, music, and physical education programs for the elementary grades," I said. "They cut teachers' planning periods. This isn't a district where most families can afford music lessons or art camps. It confounds me."

"That sounds like white-woman problems," Tom replied, maybe half in jest. Eyebrows raised around the table. (Hey, if your circle of covenantal friendships is full of people who only nod in assent, it's not keeping covenant with you.) "If those are priorities for your family, couldn't those be extracurricular, stuff you do at home? Why don't you just try Lansing for a year and see how it goes?"

"Can we back up—why is it a white-woman problem?" Dave came to my defense with a chuckle. And he could have added, there are plenty of nonwhite parents who value those things too.

"Because it's a privilege to choose a school based on what you value," Tom said, not unkindly. Nor untruthfully.

"Is it wrong to not choose a school because you don't like the programs the district offers?"

"No, but I think it matters less in elementary school."

"But Schools of Choice openings go way down after kinder-garten," I replied. "Holt School District only has five openings for second graders, but they have sixty-some for kindergarten. There was, like, *one* opening for high school." I rattled off the numbers I'd recently seen advertised in the newspaper.

Sounds like an awkward dinner, no? Look, it could've been. But our friendship had evolved to the level of near-family. Tom was speaking as a brother in Christ. One of the biggest gifts the year of small things offers is this: no more are our parenting de-cisions happening in a vacuum. It's also the painful part: group discernment is hard, especially when you can't use the same verbal shorthand with your friends as you do with your spouse. Your art-degree-holding husband will understand why cutting fine arts from schools is a deal-breaker; your friends may wonder if this has more to do with something else, something like poverty, racial diversity, or test scores. And you'll have to do some soul-searching: How much of this conversation is really about "good schools," and how much of it is about race, class, privilege?

Here's what you do: serve dessert. We paused as Sarah rose from
her chair to dig in the pantry. "Graham crackers? They're all I have,"
she called. "I can make some frosting too." She emerged with a
1980s-era child's cookbook and a bag of powdered sugar. A few minutes later, the kids swarmed like wasps around a runny white glaze.
"What did I do wrong? Why's it not thickening?" Sarah laughed.

"No matter—just drizzle it over the crackers. It's just sugar.
It'll be great." Dave's an encourager.

"Who wants a cracker with frost—er, icing?" Kids' hands went
in the air while a chorus of "Me!" responses rang out. The adults
reached for one too. We all licked the sides of our cracker sand-
wiches, catching the glaze.

"I want my kids to learn with people who don't look like them."
I calmly licked my fingers. "But I also want them to have access
to field trips and art and all that. Dave and I majored in the arts.
These aren't just hobbies. We orient our lives around writing and
creating."

Some heads nodded. Kids asked for seconds. Dave asked for
seconds.

"The worst part is, we don't even know where we're going to
live yet," Dave said. "This is all hypothetical."

"So, Jesus, guide us," Sarah said. Cracker crumbs lay all over
the table and on our kids' lips.

"Yes, Amen."

Sarah's Story

While Erin and Dave were wringing their hands and slipping antac-
ids this spring, you might say the Arthurs got off easy. Again. Tom
got to play prophet in residence (a slightly different hat than the
pietist one) while I stirred icing, and somehow the Wasingers didn't
end up shredding our mutual covenant and stalking out the door.

This of course points to the caliber of these folks who had vowed
to share our year of small things; when they make a commitment,

they stick with it. But more importantly, it points to the nature of covenantal friendship itself. This was not some trendy reality show where we would experiment with extreme living for a limited time while voting people off the island. This was, in effect, just one semester in a school for conversion that we hoped would continue for the rest of our lives—maybe not always in this exact incarnation, but some variation. *Sorry,* we basically told each other, *you're stuck with us for life.*

So in this month of small things for small folks, what were the Arthurs doing? One simple thing, really. We escaped to a coffee-house one Saturday morning to write a family rule.

Yes, yes, I know; Erin said that no rules exist. And, on the one hand, that's true: in the Christian journey we're not always given hard-and-fast answers to specific quandaries. But, on the other hand, if we don't create some kind of spiritual blueprint for our family life, as I said in chapter 6, outside forces will dictate everything.

This is what the early monastics discovered when they first formed communities of shared life in the desert back in the third and fourth centuries. First, they needed an abbot, a parent figure who was the recognized spiritual authority. Second, they needed some basic practices, or a rule, that gave structure to their communal existence; otherwise the monastery risked becoming a kind of fourth-century Burning Man, an anything-goes desert festival. Third, the novitiates needed overt apprenticeship in this way of life—indeed, they needed a trial run to determine if this rule was something to which they were willing to submit.

So how does all this translate to a middle-class American couple sipping chai on a Saturday morning? Well, in some ways the family, as a unique unit within the broader church, operates as a kind of monastic order (minus the celibacy part). It starts off with two people who are set apart through the rite of marriage to live into particular vows. Then, if God leads in this direction, their little "order" grows, not by evangelism or conversion, but by procreation or adoption. The parents automatically play the role of the abbot (which means "father," after all), and meanwhile the tiny novitiates require some kind of structure, clear boundaries as to how life in this communal setting will not degenerate into an episode of *Jerry Springer*.

In some ways our covenant with Dave and Erin functioned as a kind of monastic rule, and certainly we hoped our boys would continue to live into those radical Christian practices with us. Indeed, we signed their names with ours. Which raises a curious problem: the children of new monastics may be the only novitiates—other than Amish children—who did not volunteer for this life of radical Christian faith. There's no trial run for my preschooler to determine whether he will submit to the twelve marks of new monasticism; these practices are the water he swims in, the air he breathes. Without a kind of new monastic version of the Amish *rumspringa* once our sons hit "the age of accountability" (or even with it), there may be therapy in store for all of us.[9]

And yet, families have rules. That's life. And if we want to create an environment in which we give our children a decent shot at growing into the character of Christ, these new monastic "rules" stand a pretty good chance of working. The trick is to tweak them in a uniquely Arthurian way, a way that somehow fits our family's vision and sense of call. Also, Sam, now age two, can't remember any of them.

So a spring Saturday morning found the Arthur parents at a coffeehouse with notebooks and tablets in hand. (We had to drop the boys off with Sam's loving godparents, Kristin and Jeremy, to make it happen. Spiritual community to the rescue. Again.)

"Even after all this," I said, warming my hands on my cup, "I'm still not sure how new monasticism translates for small kids."

"Yeah," Tom said. "I keep thinking it would be so much easier to wait till our kids are older. Or dumb everything down for the next decade." He paused, then said with a hint of bitterness, "The sophistication of my prayer life has gone to a child's level."

I coughed with laughter. He wasn't joking. This is how pietists suffer while their children are small: their disciplined spiritual regimen gets shredded into tiny bits. "And yet," I said, attempting a stern face (I didn't study youth spiritual formation in seminary for nothing), "doing spiritual practices with children still counts. It's not somehow less spiritual. God still shows up. We can still grow more like Jesus."

"But it's hard to imagine how," he said. "New monasticism isn't offering much help here."

We paused, sipped our drinks.

"What if it's something super simple," Tom said finally, "something even a child can remember? What if . . . ," and I could almost see the gears in his brain working, "what about John Wesley's Three Simple Rules?"

And that's when it clicked. John Wesley's our guy. We're Methodists, after all.[10] We like to be methodical, but we're not going to require doctoral degrees to make our methods accessible. And it doesn't get much simpler than Three Simple Rules, which can be summarized as (1) do no harm, (2) do good, and (3) stay in love with God.[11]

We started scribbling furiously. I made three columns, one for each simple rule. And underneath, the details of our family "order," loosely based on the twelve marks of new monasticism, various Wesleyan "works of piety" and "works of mercy," our experiences at Isaiah House, and these last five years of parenting. The key question was, how are we going to share Christian life together as a family, with kids? Not just *survive* life together but intentionally share a way of life that forms all of us—not just me and Tom, not just the boys—into the image of Jesus?

I can't say that what we came up with that morning was brilliant. It's mostly jargoned shorthand, reminder notes about what we sense is important for our daily and weekly communal formation. And we didn't exactly follow the monastic pattern of staying marinated in Scripture all day, all week, which is the single most striking thing about the old monastic orders. They didn't have long, elaborate lists of dos and don'ts, just regular patterns of reciting and singing Scripture. (If we manage once a day at bedtime, we're doing well. Once is better than never.) But it's a blueprint, one we can take with us as the boys grow older, something we can sit down with year after year and ask each other, "How are we doing? What needs to change?" And then when the tough decisions come, when it's time to rein in a wandering teenager or respond to a job offer, for instance, we will have been practicing the art of communal discernment all along the way.

One snapshot of how this has played out since that coffeehouse date: Under "Do no harm," I scribbled the eleventh mark of new monasticism—"peacemaking in the midst of violence and conflict resolution along the lines of Matthew 18." Our basic assumption is that peacemaking starts at home, with your immediate community. In other words, I will be really ticked off if my sons are at the state capitol staging nonviolent protests over racial profiling but have not sought reconciliation with each other over a girl (or insert your area of grown sibling conflict here).

This means, while the boys are still small, Tom and I model confession and forgiveness, *adult to adult*. For example, "I'm sorry I snapped at you before dinner, Tom. Will you forgive me?" followed by Tom saying, "I forgive you" (not, "It's okay"—because it's not okay). More importantly, we model confession and forgiveness, *adult to child*. For example, "I'm sorry I snapped at you before dinner, Micah. Will you forgive me?" which prompts Micah to say, "I forgive you"—plus a wet kiss on the cheek for effect (his idea). And most importantly, we encourage the boys to confess and ask forgiveness of *each other*—not merely, "Say you're sorry," because that asks nothing of the wounded party in return. The wounded party needs to learn how to forgive just as much as the wounder needs to learn to confess.

(And let's be honest: hearing my two-year-old lisp, "I foh-give you, Micah John," makes me want to weep big, sappy monastic tears.)

Small steps. A weird mash-up of Wesleyan monasticism, at the preschool level. But as the boys grow older, they can help us craft this rule to fit the various seasons in our lives.

So what about your family? It's worth acknowledging here that genuine pietists come along roughly twice a millennium, and I happen to be married to one of them (the other being the founder of Methodism). As Erin reminded me, most of us will not be writing elaborate family rules and pulling them out every time the children try to stab each other with sporks over who gets the first hot dog. But you can write the Three Simple Rules and put them on the fridge. Or to make it more personal, you can write a family mission statement, just one line that starts with "We exist to . . ." This week, consider finishing that sentence together—make it concrete, such as, "We exist to share the love of Jesus with strangers," or "We exist to glorify God and enjoy him forever" (thank you, Westminster Shorter Catechism). Keep it short. Then put it on the fridge; bring it out at dinnertime; use it when you have a big decision to make.

And the next time you get together with those covenantal friends, ask them to ask you how your mission is going. Have you done harm this week? Have you done good? Are you staying in love with God?

Am I? Are you?

Back to Erin

The Arthurs drank chai. We waited and we prayed, waited and prayed. When the kids would ask where we'd live, where they'd go to school, we'd say, "God will tell us when we need to know."

And then we *did* know where we would live. The week after we made the accepted offer, we called the small elementary school a couple of blocks away from what would be our new home.

"Can we have a tour?" I asked, much to the surprise of the principal on the other end.

"Oh, yeah. Anytime. Just come on over," she said warmly. So we did.

We wore our winter coats that blustery, gray spring day. "Arts. Athletics. Achievement. Lansing School District." Dave and I looked at the banner waving in the wind, then at each other.

"Erin—don't," he warned. "Open minds, remember?"

I bit my lip. I prayed God would open my imagination.

We walked the halls, glancing in classroom doorways and out a window to the playground. A paraprofessional pointed out attributes: teachers who'd been there for years; students who attended from all over the district. The school was fine; it could have been Anywhere Elementary. But there was no flash of insight, not even a small flicker. We thanked our hosts and left in silence.

The same night, I slapped a stack of Schools of Choice applications on the kitchen island. The papers slid across the Formica. "This is just a huge decision," I said. "We need more time." On the edge of the counter was a box of books and homeschooling supplies I was selling to a friend. I'd jammed the abacus beside a book about martyrs and a collection of fables. These were not things I was letting go of lightly. For two solid years our family had been immersed in a particular philosophy of education; our home *was* our school. The switch to public education was, all by itself, a huge adjustment. "Let's apply for Schools of Choice, just to buy us time to think about it."

"So we just wait to decide, then?" Dave leaned against the counter. I loathed the wait, but we needed time to pray, to be silent before God about this one.

"Let's wait. Sending in the application for Holt schools lets us not decide anything for a while," I said. "If we don't get in to Holt, we'll have our answer."

"Okay," Dave said, yawning. "Let's watch some Netflix. I can't think about this anymore."

•••••

A couple of weeks into July, we got the call: "Yes, I show Alice and Violet both got in to Sycamore Elementary School in Holt," said the woman on the other end.

At this point you're wondering if any other tree does, in fact, grow in Michigan. But there's a kind of poetry here: the same creek that flows just east of our church and our own urban neighborhood winds its way south into the suburbs. Also, we'd done our homework: Sycamore Elementary is a suburban school, but it's a diverse elementary in the Holt district. Its student body resembles our Lansing neighborhood socioeconomically and demographically. About half of Sycamore students qualify for free or reduced-price lunches. Additionally, it runs on the balanced calendar, which for us is compelling: students learn for five or six weeks, then get a week or two off—an echo of the Sabbath. So the call came. We exhaled. Tom and Sarah prayed and cheered. And then we did all the normal school things: the paperwork, buying the lunch boxes, the new shoes. The girls transitioned to public school with only a few tears, and we have peace about it because the decision feels settled for now. Months of discernment granted us peace—for now.

Looking back, I believe our grossest error this spring wasn't enrolling in a suburban school. It was viewing new monasticism as a "must be this tall to ride" stick at an amusement park; we wondered if applying for a suburban district was like abandoning the roller coaster queue to hop on the toddler train. This, of course, is the opposite of the freedom and joy that should come from a life of faith. Over and over, we need to be reminded by covenantal friends that we can be firm in claiming that Jesus "saved us, not because of the righteous things *we* had done, but because of *his* mercy" (Titus 3:5 NLT, my emphasis); our spiritual merit badges are meaningless (see 3:9). In the end, there's only the grace offered to us by Jesus.

•••••

We're not done discerning. When I sit behind the wheel of my van waiting for the 3:30 p.m. bell in the pickup line at Sycamore

Elementary, "absurd," "hypocritical," "peculiar," and "scared white woman" are among the nicer words I use to describe myself. We're advocating for being in relationships with those outside our racial and ethnic enclave . . . but here we sit, idling in a suburban school's carpool line. I hear a desert father's admonition: "Teach your heart to follow what your tongue is saying to others."[12] Darn those fathers who weren't actually fathers.

So we pray for grace.

Perhaps Schools of Choice was the grace that inspired us to move to Lansing; maybe people can choose a struggling city but not necessarily its schools. Or maybe we have the grace of time. Who knows? When Alice ages out of Sycamore Elementary after fourth grade, we may have relationships in our neighborhood that make Lansing schools the obvious choice.

What this process *hasn't* granted us is indifference. We've wrestled like Jacob with this decision so long our hips ache; we'll forever walk with a limp (see Gen. 32:22–32). The dirt around our feet is scuffed as if we'd dug in our heels to fight. When Lansing cut elementary arts programs, it hurt like the cut was personal. As we're grafted to this neighborhood, we share this injury (see Heb. 13:3). We're never going to be "over" the Schools of Choice conversation because too deeply ingrained is our call not to abandon what the Empire's neglected.

We weren't ready to have our kids walk in front of us, carrying the new monastic banner, but we as adults can't *not* engage here. This means we don't volunteer our time in suburban schools; we volunteer in Lansing schools. More on this in chapter 12, but be warned: when two artists get righteously angry, we're most likely to want to create something beautiful, and we're doing that with a middle school in Lansing right now.

Maybe it's here that you can begin to wonder with me: How can we navigate the decisions we make about our children so that we're making decisions not just for the happiness of our nuclear unit but for the wholeness of the families who live on our block?

How can we begin to locate the hopes we have for our own children within the same breath as the hopes we have for all of our city's children? Are we brave enough to discern this stuff with our friends and our church? How can our churches be in relationship with those around them so that it's impossible for us to claim ignorance? Are we flexible enough to admit that God might change our minds about our decisions later? Can we see how an openness to the marks of new monasticism is a gift, not a wall too high for those with children—or for the children themselves—to climb?

The practices of radical faith must be a gift, because if we're only offering rules, we're woefully on the wrong path. Grace—let's be good at grace.

Questions for Reflection and Discussion

1. What decisions have others helped you discern? How has that shaped your thinking process?
2. If you're a parent, what do you want for your children's education? How does this influence your family's choices about where to live or which schools your children will attend? Are there negative consequences to making those choices?
3. If you have children, how do they shape your interpretation of new monasticism?
4. Pencil out a family rule. Plan to revisit it often as a couple, and then with your children as they get older. How will you know, years from now, whether you stayed on target?

For Further Reading

Miller-McLemore, Bonnie J. *Let the Children Come: Reimagining Childhood from a Christian Perspective.* San Francisco: Jossey-Bass, 2003.

Robinson, David. *The Busy Family's Guide to Spirituality: Practical Lessons for Modern Living from the Monastic Tradition.* New York: Crossroad, 2009.

Sider, Ronald J. *Just Politics: A Guide for Christian Engagement.* Grand Rapids: Brazos, 2012.

This American Life. Episode 562, "The Problem We All Live With." July 31, 2015. http://www.thisamericanlife.org/radio-archives/episode/562/transcript.

10

sustaining creation

I don't think things can be made perfect all the way—
I mean, shalom is not fully possible—until Christ's
return. But we should get started on some of the work
so Dad isn't mad when he gets back.

—Erin Wasinger

Sarah's Story

"Quick, Micah," I said, thrusting a bucket at my preschooler and motioning toward the door. "See how many dandelions you can pick before Daddy comes home. I'll pay you a penny apiece."

"Really?" he said. "Great!" He glanced toward the counter at the chore money in his give-save-spend jars and headed for the door. Pausing on the front porch that sparkling May afternoon, he gazed at the sunny lawn. "Whoa. That's a lot of dandelions."

"Yep," I said. "Just don't say that to Daddy."

"Okay." He leapt down the steps and set to work. As I folded socks while Sam napped, I could see Micah dashing excitedly, haphazardly, from clump to clump around our enormous corner lot. Ten minutes later, he tromped back through the door, flush with pride and sunshine.

He plopped the overflowing bucket down. "I'm done."

It was then I realized two flaws in my plan. First, I would have to count every darn dandelion (in the end I owed him $2.60). And second, an enthusiastic preschooler armed with a bucket and financial incentive had made no observable dent in our lawn-care situation. And by "situation" I mean like when a TV cop shows up at a crime scene and says into a radio, "We have a situation here."

By suburban standards, the new crop of bright yellow flowers that had appeared at sunrise (despite Tom's dutiful mowing the evening prior) was a situation. It was, in fact, an ongoing situation: a six-year-long passive-aggressive battle between our neighborhood and us that Tom referred to, between clenched teeth, as the Dandelion Wars.

It had begun shortly after our arrival in Michigan as a simple complaint—yes, someone actually complained to the neighborhood association about our lawn care (or what they perceived as a lack thereof). We were tempted to put a sign on the grass that said, "For the health of your pets, your children, the earth, and your reproductive organs, this grass has not been treated with pesticides. You're welcome." And we could have added, "Oh, and if your lawn is not a huge corner lot visible from all sides without the privacy of trees and shrubs, then shut up."

But we didn't. We simply refused, stubbornly, to treat the parsonage lawn with pesticides.[1]

This was not an arbitrary decision. It was born out of a deeply theological, intentionally countercultural conviction that this plot of soil matters, that we are called to care for this earth God has given us. It's only by our treating creation sustainably that creation, by God's providence, can sustain us.

New monastics weren't the first to influence us in this practice, although we wholeheartedly embrace their emphasis on "care for the plot of God's earth given to us along with support of our local economies." No, this was a conviction that Tom had gleaned early on and carried into our married life. I often say I'm an environmentalist by marriage; thanks in part to his influence, I started recycling, started paying attention to the chemicals I use, began shopping at the local co-op (where, not incidentally, my sister works).[2] Throughout our first decade together, Tom attended composting classes, volunteered with the local watershed council, and mowed our tiny lot in Petoskey with an old-fashioned push mower. He joined the Sierra Club, researched our carbon footprint, and was genuinely shaken when one website calculated that if every person on the planet lived as we did, it would take three earths to support our current lifestyle. For more than a dozen years we'd had just one car.

When I say Tom gleaned these convictions early, I mean there's something in his genetic makeup that gives elements of his maternal family a radically countercultural proclivity in this area. This is not to be taken lightly, as Erin learned the hard way. She casually mentioned the documentary *Food, Inc.* once in conversation, complaining about the seemingly unattainable yet intriguing ideals of Joel Salatin, the famous ecological chicken farmer featured in the film.

"Actually," Tom said, "he's my cousin."

Well, technically, Joel Salatin is Tom's mom's cousin. Joel had become famous long before *Food, Inc.* through his renegade farming practices (one of his more popular book titles is *Everything I Want to Do Is Illegal*). But he had rocketed into celebrity status thanks to Michael Pollan's best seller *The Omnivore's Dilemma: A Natural History of Four Meals*, in which Pollan traces meals back to their original sources and explores the processes that bring those meals to our tables. When Tom read that book years ago, he said, "Whenever we're out east, we need to visit the Salatins' farm."

So in our final year in North Carolina, we did just that. After meeting us in person at the funeral of Tom's grandmother in Indiana, the Salatins invited us and the members of Isaiah House to stay in Virginia for a weekend. Over several days we toured Polyface Farm, drank raw milk at breakfast, ate our fill of free-range beef and pork (and the only bacon and ribs I'd ever seen my vegetarian housemate Rebecca eat), and sat at the proverbial feet of the man we dubbed the Prophet Joel.[3]

Here's a snapshot of that visit, to give you an idea of how deep this runs for Tom: Joel had just taken us around the farm, from the portable chicken coop up to the shimmery, grassy pastures and back down again to the open barn, where he vaulted effortlessly into the pigpen. His enthusiasm for honoring "the pigness of the pig" could not have been more contagious; we all wanted to jump in there with him.[4] With his big farmer's hands Joel reached down, grabbed a pile of manure, thrust it joyfully at us, and said, "Smell that!" We smelled it. It was like no manure I'd ever encountered— and as a kid in central New York State I'd lived next door to cows for several years. It was almost not a smell, in the negative sense, but some robust, healthy combination of spring dirt, sweet corn, and . . . the only description that seems to fit: happy pig.

"Do you smell that?" he asked, grinning.

We nodded. Pigness.

There in front of us was proof of what we had learned in our seminary Old Testament classes: that God, the people, and the land form a triangle of interconnected relationships. The Hebrew word for "man"—*adam*—in Genesis 2:7 comes from *adamah*, or "dust of the ground"; so that verse reads, "Then the LORD God formed [*adam*] from the [*adamah*], and breathed into his nostrils the breath [or spirit, *ruach*] of life." Human, earth, and God, bound together in vital relationship. Which means that when one of those relationships suffers, the others do too. When we devastate the land through chemicals or strip-mining or suburban sprawl, when we violate "the pigness of the pig" through mass production, something happens to our connection with God—and also to our essential humanity. When we demean other human beings through unfair wages and labor practices (a signature flourish of big agriculture), we deny not only God's spirit of life in them but their *adamah*, their very earth-ness, their createdness. And when we rebel against God by failing to acknowledge God's lordship, creation itself groans, waiting for our redemption (see Rom. 8:19–23).

Conversely, when we repent and turn back to God—according to the original, biblical prophet Joel—the land itself rejoices. In the book that bears Joel's name, the land is overrun by locusts. And God doesn't command the people to develop a new kind of pesticide but rather tells them to fast, to weep, to "return to me" (Joel 2:12). Even the ground itself mourns (1:10). But eventually, Joel says,

> Then the LORD became jealous for his *land*,
> and had pity on his *people*.
> (2:18, emphasis added)

The Lord speaks words of comfort to his people and promises restoration (see 2:19), but he also says, "Do not fear, O soil" (2:21) and "Do not fear, you animals of the field" (2:22). Whatever humans have done to you by their disobedience, O earth, let it be known that you—as well as their own humanity—can be restored.

This is not to deny that Jesus is the ultimate restorer. We still need the Son of Man (of *adam*, remember) to go down into the earthen *adamah* of the tomb and then emerge triumphant to usher in the final healing of all things. Indeed, it's no wonder that Mary Magdalene mistook her risen Lord for a gardener (see John 20:15); the same Lord, the original Gardener who walked in Eden in the cool of the day, now stood before her (see Gen. 3:8). If our call is to imitate Christ, to become more and more like him, then the fact that his resurrected body looked suspiciously like someone who works the soil should give us a clue about our redemptive task.

Do you see how deep this goes? When you claim this kind of prophetic vision about the created order of things—about the God-human-land sacredness of something so ordinary and yet so culturally invisible as a pig—when that kind of fiery passion is buried in your DNA, you are not going to take something like suburban dandelions lightly.

Nor anything else in the nonsustainable environmental practices of American suburbia, for that matter. The dandelions were emblematic of a larger war—a war in which Tom felt like we were slowly losing ground, year after year.

Take transportation, for instance. At first we were determined to stick with just one car, to lighten our carbon footprint, despite the fact that we lived in the southern subdivision farthest from the city. Tom attempted biking to work for a while, but between the lack of bike lanes and arriving exhausted—not to mention persistent back problems exacerbated by a car accident—he eventually gave it up.[5] We're grateful that our subdivision benefits from the tail end of the city bus line, which allowed me to run errands even with Micah in tow. I learned much about south Lansing's demographics—including the fact that there's such a thing as the "suburban poor"—by hopping on the number 8.[6] And many kind people loaned us cars, including our parents. But between Michigan winters, Tom's schedule, and my second pregnancy, it became clear that this was not going to cut it for long. By the time Sam arrived, we owned a second car.

Water usage was another battle, one that we lost almost instantly. Granted, we had just come from the drought-plagued Southeast, where people were ticketed for watering their lawns or washing their cars, so our habits (like placing a bucket under the shower head to collect water for flushing the toilet, not letting the water run while brushing teeth, not using the dishwasher) could be construed as extreme. Okay, so we were weirdos. Our church members were awfully kind about it, but we could tell they thought we were hilarious. And after the spring rains, I understood. The

Grand River system—which is most of Lansing—is a flood zone. As soon as the snows melted that first year, our backyard became a pond. When the sump pump failed, Tom frantically dashed to the store and bought a temporary pump, which he hooked up to the garden hose—which we then threaded out the basement window. The next morning, I looked outside to see mallards swimming in my backyard.

Are you keeping a tally? There's more. The failed community garden in our subdivision. The Amish CSA (community-supported agriculture) share that ended abruptly when that particular farmer no longer distributed to our local market. The fact that we now ran the dishwasher at least once a day. And a thousand other small losses, a thousand trillion dandelions.

Those dandelions. Poor Tom. Several years into our new life here, after finally giving in and admitting that, yes, the dandelions were becoming a problem, he researched an organic, sustainable process that would give us, in his words, "the best damn lawn in the neighborhood." It was expensive. And time-consuming. It involved things like raking in compost and dethatching and overseeding and bagging and watering (we had plenty of water now, remember). Our neighbors simply had no categories for responding to this: one woman, walking briskly by as we raked yards of compost into the grass, shook her head and said, "That just doesn't look fun, guys." (Well, um . . .) But our busy schedules, a shrinking budget, and a second baby left us almost no margin to keep it up. This May found us almost back where we started.

"Dad!" Micah yelled as Tom walked through the door. "I picked dandelions and made two dollars and sixty cents!"

"Yeah?" Tom said, glancing outside. A pause. A sag to the shoulders. He bent down and kissed the top of Micah's head. "Great job, buddy."

Later that evening, as Tom and I chatted in bed before prayer time, we returned to the conundrum that continued to trouble us. That is, living simply and living sustainably are not necessarily the same things. Giving in to suburbia's way of handling lawn care would be simple. It would be cheaper. It would take less time. It would make our neighbors smile with gratitude. But living sustainably, by contrast, seemed like some unattainable luxury of the leisure class. The expense, the time, the agency to do what you choose with your own land . . . How on earth (short of moving, which was up to the bishop, not us) were we supposed to care for this plot of—well . . . earth?

While we wrestled with this seemingly insurmountable problem, Erin and Dave, by contrast—whose impending move made their life complicated on many levels—managed to take one simple step.

Erin's Story

"Pass me your debit card." I sat on the love seat, laptop on my legs. "Please."

"Why?" Dave drew out his card anyway, as he drew out the question.

"We're getting a CSA share this year," I announced. It was ten o'clock at night as I typed in the details that moved a hundred bucks from our bank to a farm twenty minutes away.

"Okay, sounds good," he said. "I've been wanting to do that for years."

"Well, here you go: victory." I shut down the computer, and we prayed. We switched off the lamp and navigated the tricky path to our bedroom, stubbing toes on the corners of moving boxes stacked along the hallway. Voilà! Creation care: check.

It took you longer to read those paragraphs than it took us to discern our small practice in caring for this planet. This was May, remember. We'd just made an offer on a house in Lansing. We were still talking about schooling options. The dog, who hates moving boxes, was puking in corners of the living room. No, I didn't have the headspace to start a garden with someone, get one of those upside-down tomato-growing apparatuses, or plan seasonal meals.

There is a time for everything, Ecclesiastes 3:2 tells us: a time to plant and a time to harvest. The year we bought a house was not either of those times.

The beauty of community-supported agriculture is this: We pay a fee up front for a small family farm to provide us with fresh veggies, fruits, herbs, and (if we want) eggs and cheese weekly throughout the six-month growing season. In return, the family earns a fair wage, avoids pesticides, and harvests sustainable crops. We both win. As any farmer will attest, farming is a mixed bag. My stepdad, who grows soybeans, corn, and wheat in Ohio, watched in horror this same spring and summer as his fields sat underwater. (Farming is a spiritual discipline.) The farmer is completely at the mercy of the whims of weather. Community-supported agriculture says, "We're here for you, rain or drought. We value your vocation; we value your land and how you choose to farm it."

Of course, we're not entirely selfless here. We get fresher produce than when we shop at the big-box store down the street. This matters for so many reasons: selfishly, it just tastes better when our potatoes and tomatoes haven't been hauled to Michigan from California in the back of a truck; the carbon impact of our food is so small when you take out that cross-country commute; and (this is a big one) we know who grows and harvests our food. Volunteers help us count vegetables on pickup dates at another CSA member's home in Lansing. Plus, what an adventure to get vegetables we wouldn't buy at the grocery store! I was amazed at the green, bumpy saber-looking things: I'm not sure how I thought brussels sprouts grew, but it certainly wasn't that way. Some vegetables were abominable. (My forefathers left Germany so we wouldn't have to eat rutabagas.) And, terrifyingly, I began to realize we were subsidizing the production of kale. (*It tastes like feet.* And, yes, I've tried kale chips.)

Our experience wasn't all bad. Dozens of shades of red tomatoes lined our counter for more than two months. For a blessed week in the summer, we got pints of blueberries and bags of

Michigan peaches—oh, a Michigan peach! Poetry in my mouth.
We scrubbed fresh baby potatoes, tossing them in oil and grilling
them up beside our veggie burgers. Summer was tasty, and those
tastes were local.

Did it make a difference to our grocery budget? It did not. Will
we do it again? I'd love to instead plant some of our favorite foods
in a raised bed in our backyard, and now that we're within biking
distance of a couple of farmers' markets, I'd rather buy what we
like (less kale) as we need it. CSA boxes aren't perfect, but they
are one way we who don't reside in the country can support those
who grow our food. As Eric Jacobsen writes in *Sidewalks in the
Kingdom*, those of us who live on land that's not growing food
should be supporting the local economies that do.[7] Bonus points
if you know the names of those who keep giving you all those
potatoes, tomatoes, and berries (thank you, Titus Farms).

The CSA experience reminded us that our small-scale food
decisions matter. Lugging home a haul on a Wednesday night
was a lesson in local agriculture, an attempt to resolve our initial helplessness after hearing the sustainable-food rallying cry
of *Food, Inc.* This is one way to take your big-agriculture angst
and turn it into food on the table; I need not raise and de-feather
my own chicken dinner! Further, we had so many conversations,
Dave and I, about our meat consumption (because Americans
consume way too much,[8] and bacon is a meat, and we love, love,
love bacon), our cravings for off-season or nonregional produce
(Is that kiwi a treat or a staple? How about those bananas?),[9] and
our treatment of the land in our care—our plot of land and our
city's.

Where can you get your hands dirty? If you can't commit to
gardening or don't have the space, support those who do through
a CSA or a produce stand.

And get to know the seasons where you live. This far north,
fruit is our first lesson in listening to the earth instead of our
cravings. Alice was barely two years old when Dave hauled her

to the first U-pick strawberry patch in late May; what I thought was sunburn was juice smeared all over her grinning face. We go from making jam around Memorial Day to rhubarb crisp in June. We pick blueberries with friends in July. When the farmers' market stops selling watermelon, we mourn its season passing. Mom's zucchinis line our countertops every August; her spaghetti squash creeps out a child or two in early fall. The kids and I talk about the long journeys our bananas take, and why we don't buy raspberries in December.

This sounds so simple as to be ridiculous, but buying locally grown produce is difficult to do without some intention. The chain grocer will always sell watermelon; this is weird. Stop and consider how. Consider the Michigan-ness of the Michigan-grown asparagus or your region's equivalent. Sure, we often buy carrots, celery, and grapes that grew with no Midwestern sunshine; we're a family of five—I can't convert the garage into a greenhouse to feed us. But in what ways is it possible to reduce our reliance on the long-distance relationship we have with food?

Farmers' markets are perfect places to begin. The guy who lives in your county knows much more about the crop of potatoes he's selling than the cashier at the supermarket. Make it a game: Can you buy only local meat, eggs, and produce for a month?[10] Can you go meatless most nights for dinner?

Can you fill your freezer with enough blueberries in July to make it through the winter? How much of the produce can you use rather than tossing all the scraps? Can you roast the squash seeds? Plant them? Turn them to compost? A friend of ours attempted to turn all of his family's food waste into compost—using worms. He built a plastic contraption of stacked concentric circles of worms (in their basement! worms! how did his wife agree to this?) that was the highlight of a tour of their home. "The tomatoes that grow using this soil—" he said, ecstasy on his face, "oh, man. Just, oh man."

Oh, *adam*, he might've said. Oh *adamah*.

Back to Sarah

"Hey, is someone going to be around the farm this morning?" I messaged my friend Marilyn a few days after Micah cashed in big on dandelions. "I'd like to come get some composted manure, if that's okay."

"Come on over!" she messaged back.

The Manninos are longtime members of Sycamore Creek Church who live just south of Michigan State University's vast agricultural farms. They also happen to have, like Tom, that renegade streak. The Manninos are small-scale farmers who work other jobs too, but their horses, chickens, vegetable garden, and front acreage of hay (which they grow to feed the horses) makes their place one of our boys' favorites.

Even though this adventure would take far more time and coordination than simply running up to the hardware store for some Miracle-Gro for the kitchen garden, in this instance I was determined to care for creation more than I cared for my calendar. We still hadn't figured out what to do about the dandelions. Maybe we never would. But here was one small thing we *could* do. Maybe not "simple" (as in, easy), but certainly more sustainable.

I emptied Micah's dandelion bucket of fluff (carefully, into one of those big brown leaf bags) and threw it in the back of the car, along with a bunch of other buckets and a shovel. Then I buckled in the boys. Soon we were backing up to the Manninos' pasture as Joe Sr. and Joe Jr. emerged from the house to greet us.

This was not our first visit. We had a tradition now: Joe Sr. took Sam in his arms and walked him around on a baby-friendly tour, talking gently about those silly chickens, keeping an eye on the roving rooster. I, meanwhile, worked alongside Joe Jr. and Micah, filling buckets with what another renegade friend from church reverently refers to as "holy crap" (he uses another word, but you get the point).

As Micah dug in, I watched my preschooler, this little son of Adam, working the *adamah*. I watched him measure out that holy soil, aim for the bucket, miss, try again. And I realized that this small thing was part of a bigger story going all the way back to the prophet Joel, back even to Genesis. By digging into this dirt, my little human was participating in God's restoration of that broken triad: God, *adam*, *adamah*. Creation sustaining my son, my son sustaining creation, God sustaining us all. When, with our resurrected bodies, we get to join the Gardener in the healing that is the new creation, my son's muscles will remember the grip on the shovel, the heft of the soil, a good day's work.

We went home, spread composted manure in the kitchen garden, and dug some more. We made lines in the soil with sticks, poured spinach and kale seeds into recycled yogurt cups, pressed those seeds into the ground. Never mind that planting seeds with small children can be a harrowing experience not particularly guaranteed for success. Ignore, too, that Erin *will not touch* the final result, even should every other food supply on earth be cut off, world without end, amen. We were participating in some small way in God's sustaining of all things.

And it was good.

～～～ *Questions for Reflection and Discussion* ～～～

1. Where do you see the broken triad of relationship between God, humans, and the earth? Where do you see signs of restoration?

2. What has been your experience of caring for God's creation?

3. Like the Arthurs, do you see tensions between living simply and living sustainably? How might those tensions be resolved?

4. What small thing could you begin doing to better care for God's creation?

For Further Reading

Berry, Wendell. *The Mad Farmer Poems.* New York: Counterpoint, 2008.

———. *Sabbaths.* San Francisco: North Point Press, 1987.

———. *What Are People For? Essays.* San Francisco: North Point Press, 1990. See also other books, essays, poems, and stories by Wendell Berry.

Davis, Ellen F. *Scripture, Culture, and Agriculture: An Agrarian Reading of the Bible.* Cambridge: Cambridge University Press, 2008.

The Green Bible (NRSV). New York: HarperOne, 2008.

Kingsolver, Barbara. *Animal, Vegetable, Miracle: A Year of Food Life.* New York: HarperCollins, 2007.

McMinn, Lisa Graham. *To the Table: A Spirituality of Food, Farming, and Community.* Grand Rapids: Brazos, 2016.

Wirzba, Norman. *Food and Faith: A Theology of Eating.* Cambridge: Cambridge University Press, 2011.

11

unselfish self-care

From a theological perspective, the most dangerous
thing about mental illness is that it can lock us in ourselves, convincing us that we are indeed our own, and
completely on our own, isolated in our distress.

—Kathryn Greene-McCreight[1]

Erin's Story

I found a folded-up card on my desk one morning in early June:
"Deer Mom," she wrote in marker, above two stick people. One
was wearing hipster glasses, so I assume that was me. Inside: "I
hope you feel better soon. Love, Alice." I flipped back to the cover,
trying to jog my memory: When had I been sick? When did she
slip this here, amid my library books and my notes?

Alice's newly seven-year-old frame appeared tall in the doorway.
"I made that for you."

"I see that. Thank you—when did you give this to me?"

"When you were in the shower." So a few minutes ago.

"Why?"

She shrugged. I thought over the morning. The girls were fighting over a jar of marbles. I'd locked myself in the bedroom, staring at the ceiling. I showered and stood under the spray, and the fan and the water drowned out the girls' voices. I sighed over and over. That's how I know depression is worsening: I sigh all the time; my lungs expel little puffs of wordless prayers. There are the familiar signs too: The effort to rise from bed is herculean. I put away the complicated recipes. We subsist on grilled cheese or tacos for dinner, until the kids beg for something different, like frozen pizza. I'm emotionally numb; smiling becomes no longer spontaneous but instead a labor I talk myself through, coercing my facial muscles to act natural. My voice changes; its timbre becomes weak. Even my esophagus feels tired.

I know this beast, this illness. We've been in an on-and-off relationship for a decade and a half.

I hugged Alice. "Mom's going through a rough time. I don't feel well."

She pulled away abruptly. "Are you going to throw up?" She's no Florence Nightingale, this one.

"No."

"Okay. Can I go outside?"

I nodded.

The receptionist at the doctor's office picked up her phone before Alice slammed the front door. "I need to make an appointment. Erin W-a-s-i-n-g-e-r," I said. "Depression," I answered.

The beast has a name.

•••••

Can you say its name? I've learned to. But in the church, in Christian community, mental illness may well be That Which Shall Not Be Named. Mentioning it is awkward; explaining symptoms is hard.

Actually, in this conversation about radical faith, just bringing up the care of our physical, emotional, and mental well-being sounds disjointed, maybe even kind of secular self-helpy. We're supposed to be out there with the poor and the poor in spirit, right? We're supposed to be digging our hands into the earthiness of the earth, celebrating creation. We're supposed to be sharing life and worshiping and praying together, and this is supposed to fill us with radiant joy, which always translates to perfect cholesterol, blemish-free skin, and luminously white smiles. We're supposed to be making casseroles for our neighbors, not talking about how many calories those casseroles have or when we last went on a long run or how that antidepressant is helping us sleep. Those problems are so first world! Come on. When you're doing God's will, everything else just falls into place, right?

Much as we love to believe that, part of our conviction about God dwelling in us and being at work around us requires us to take care of the temple he's lent us— and to help others take care of themselves too. When one in the community is not well (and chances are you're practicing hospitality with someone who is, in some way, not well), the whole community feels it. While the support of a community is a blessing to those who suffer, the entire community struggles under the weight of what's not working— that's why we need to acknowledge what we're all carrying.

Name the beast, friends.

●♦●●●

So in June, right in the middle of our epic move from rural to urban America, I went on an antidepressant (again, after two years off). I suppose it was good timing, from a practical standpoint, since we were talking about self-care anyway—but really, who likes practical standpoints? I'd planned to use my section of this chapter to talk about running as a physical and mental discipline, warning about the trendy running culture that takes what is good and lures us into spending exorbitant amounts of energy (and money) analyzing our pace, distance, gait, and gear. Instead, I was swallowing a yellow pill every morning, my abnormally low serotonin levels shooting sky-high. I felt nauseated yet artificially happy. ("Is this how everyone else feels all the time? This is *awesome*," I told my doctor a few weeks after I started. "You'll get used to it," she replied. She was right. My emotions leveled out and became my own again as my body adjusted to the medicine.)

We don't get to choose the ways our bodies will respond to the potent biology-and-circumstances cocktail in our lives. We only get to decide what to do after we're diagnosed. Dave and our covenantal friends loved me enough not to pressure me—but now that I'm back on solid ground, I do wish they would've asked me to talk to my doctor long before Alice wrote me that card. But it's hard to hold someone accountable to his or her own well-being. How do you talk to someone about their health—especially their mental health? (For the record, "Hey, I've been noticing you're kind of a basket case lately" has never gone over really well.)

I'm not advocating that we abdicate our responsibility for our own well-being. Instead, I'm advocating that we be proactive in our self-care by giving someone explicit permission to do some truth-telling.

Good news: holding someone accountable doesn't have to be a hostile confrontation. Consider Elijah. If there's a biblical story about depression (other than the story of Job, Jeremiah, Hannah . . .), Elijah's the guy. He's escaping someone who wants him dead; he flees to Mount Sinai, where he's at the limits of his endurance. He's struggling; he's spent. He even prays that he might die: "I have had enough, LORD," he says in 1 Kings 19:4 (NLT). (I know what it feels like to have had enough.) And then he lies down and sleeps under that broom tree. (Oh, that sleep. I know that sleep.)

We'd do well to mimic God's response to Elijah's despair when we're trying to help someone with mental illness—or any ailment, for that matter. The Spirit doesn't show up, demanding that our friend repent of his melodrama. The Spirit doesn't list a hundred reasons that Elijah should be joyful ("Look at that sunset, Elijah. That is a *nice* sunset. Who can feel sad when he's looking at a sunset?"). The Spirit doesn't ask if Elijah's carrying around unconfessed sin; God doesn't ask how Elijah's Bible-reading plan is going. An angel doesn't show up to offer five easy steps to beat the blechs. The angel doesn't remind Elijah of people in this world who would give their right arms to have what Elijah has.

Instead, an angel feeds the prophet warm bread and gives him water. Elijah then sleeps some more, and when the angel comes back, again with bread and water, the angel encourages Elijah to eat more, "or the journey ahead will be too much for you" (1 Kings 19:7 NLT). Our merciful God feeds us, tells us to rest, warns us we're not done yet. Don't rush over this part: Eat, rest, replenish your soul, or the journey will be too hard for you, friend. When God's servant said he'd had enough, God simply fed him and let him nap. Only then was he prepared to descend the mountain and continue his ministry.

Christians can look further into this story: Jesus is living water (see John 4:10), the bread of life (John 6:48). I have found Jesus in the places where I've said, "I've had enough. I don't want to die, but, Jesus, am I tired." But let's not miss the wisdom in simply allowing ourselves to rest, to eat some warm bread, to be still. Pause. Take care of yourself, or you won't be fit to join God on the other adventures planned for you.

This is the unspoken but powerful side of the new monastic quest to nurture common life and strive for disciplined, contemplative lives. Just as the Sabbath reminds us that the world will continue to spin without us if we take a break, the communal life should be asking those of us who struggle with mental illness or physical pains if it's not time to have a seat around our table and tear off some warm bread together, with our church and our covenantal community. Why? Because when we're that close to one another, it's hard to hide what's wrong. This was a good thing for me, every Tuesday, even if every fiber of my being wanted to pretend I wasn't slowly drowning in some vague feeling of anxiety and despair. And when we're sitting shoulder to shoulder, what happens? We start to talk; we start to tell stories.

When I'm at the worst of my depression, I'm alone, and I want to be left alone, but then, not. I want to hear stories because stories move me, but I can't remember them on my own. I can't see the story arc of my own life, of God's redemption, of the places God has saved me. So when we tell stories that help us remember God's work in our lives, it's powerful. This is what pushes us to hope.

This journeying together isn't always fun. We have to warn you: if you're sharing life with someone with a mental illness, there will be times when you feel that person is just a drag. Congratulations, you are now *really sharing life*. This is hard stuff, but it's the ground in which we learn to say, "I'm bringing over dinner. And I'll throw in a load of laundry for you," or "Let me mow your grass this week." This is the relationship in which we learn what not to say; this is where we learn to listen. This too is part of our formation—and also that person's, as he or she lets us come alongside (which is also hard).

So far this year we've asked Jesus to help us redeem gift giving, reclaim the Sabbath, and sustain creation. Can we also restore a sliver of our aging, unwell bodies too? Can we admit that both aging and mental illness can allow us to receive and offer undeserved, unexpected kindness? Most certainly, though, our bodies betray the truth that we are finite. *Finite.* We are not God. Not even close. Could we who suffer even go so far as to see mental illness or our bodies' imperfections as conduits of some grace, however painfully given?

Being transparent about our struggles makes us vulnerable. We're humbled. We're on level ground with those with whom we share life. We cannot afford to be self-reliant; we cannot pretend to be anyone's savior. We cannot pretend to be in control; we're ever at the mercy of God (see Ps. 37). Perhaps our broken minds or bodies are leveling grounds where those whom we are tempted

to "serve" instead become people with whom we see eye to eye.
Lose the missionary-speak here: we're all broken; we're all in need
of redemption and healing. Recognizing that is a gift. Pretending
otherwise kills authentic friendship.

Sarah's Story

Erin's email came at lunchtime. "I'm concerned for you, friend,"
she wrote. "This pace is not sustainable, and I'm worried that it's
going to wreak its revenge on your body."

She knew.

I was way overextended. Not only was I attempting to write two
books, but I had taken on volunteer leadership of our church's
youth ministry program. And I was raising two small kids, supporting a husband in ministry, providing hospitality to someone
in need, tending a garden, attempting to fix up and sell our house
in Petoskey, and incorporating a dozen-ish new monastic practices
into my overflowing life. This went way beyond my realization
back in January that I needed to declutter my schedule and practice Sabbath; that had been a good check, a gentle touch on the
brakes. It wasn't even that my busyness had now become endear-
ingly pathological—"Silly Sarah. There you go again." This was
dangerous.

It was dangerous on two levels, and at first it was hard to say
which was more serious. First, the call from the doctor's office
after some blood work: "Cholesterol levels are high. Please come
in to discuss." I knew this. It's hereditary: my grandmother had it;
my dad has it. My maternal grandfather died of a massive heart
attack when my mom was seventeen. We are not, genetically, large
people; we generally stay active, although that's often because an
active spouse says, "Let's go." Yet in the past year Tom's regimen
of physical exercise had dropped to almost nothing, which meant
mine was, if possible, less than nothing. I chased children around
the house. I pulled weeds in the garden and sometimes pushed a

wheelbarrow. I went down and back up the flight of stairs to the basement maybe twice a day, if that.

Additionally, until recently I could have said that I eat well too (while living in Isaiah House we were mostly vegetarian), but lately the daily mealtime battles with the boys just didn't seem worth it. "Fine. Eat hot dogs and grilled cheese with a side of pickles. At least you're eating." Then I'd slice myself some cheese while hovering over the cutting board, snarfing Sam's abandoned hot dog. The effort of making a salad was just too much when there were diapers in the washer, six thousand emails to answer, and spinach seeds to put in the ground (yes, I'm aware of the irony).

So until recently, my doctors would look at my blood work, discuss my other habits, and determine that I was keeping things under control through diet and exercise. But no longer.

"How many hours a week would you say you exercise?" the PA asked, glancing up from her laptop.

I shook my head.

She typed briefly. "Okay, how about diet? What kinds of things are you eating?"

Long pause. "Kid food."

"Ah . . ." More typing. Then she looked up. "You know what I'm going to say, right?"

I knew.

This was dangerous, because for most of my life I very happily would have been just a brain. Reading, writing, daydreaming, inventing, thinking, reflecting—this is what I love to do. I remember reading for hours at a stretch as a child, annoyed by the interruption of lunchtime, barely making it to the bathroom when my body finally couldn't wait any longer. I joined dance classes and sports mostly because my mom or peer pressure said, "Get up." And once I was moving, I enjoyed it, but it was not my natural inclination. When as a young adult, after nearly a decade in youth ministry, I had the chance to become a writer, I felt as if I had won the Michigan Powerball—I mean, who gets that lucky?[22] Still later, during my pregnancies, when asked, "How's it going?" I would reply, "Embodiment is not my favorite." It's not that I viewed taking care of my body as selfish—although it's a real temptation to assume the moral high ground over the woman who spends hours each week, say, getting pedicures—I just found it annoyingly inconvenient.

Now here I was, in high summer, chained to the house by the rhythms of life with small children, the demands of writing, and my own natural inclinations, and I was being told to add exercise to my already crazy to-do list. Sulking, a little scared, I hunted on Craigslist for a bike trailer—since biking is one of the rare physical activities I love—and found one in great shape for fifty dollars. Tom tuned up my bike, we strapped the helmeted boys in the trailer, and I took off with grand plans to make this the Summer of Biking Everywhere.

Sam hated it.

And the mosquitoes . . . I've already mentioned the entire Lansing region is one big swamp.

And the summer heat . . .

You can see where this is going.

Meanwhile, Tom had his own health issues—namely, trouble sleeping, something that had never plagued him before. Working furiously on his laptop straight till 10:00 p.m. prayer was not helping, nor was the lack of exercise. He eventually tackled both of these issues later in the fall by getting a gym membership, including a personal trainer, and exercising in the evenings after the boys went to bed. No screens after 9:00 p.m.; getting your butt kicked by an exercise buff who doesn't particularly care what you do for a living and has zero interest in monasticism . . . it was downright miraculous.

As Erin says, we are finite. It is not our job to save the world. Sleep is the needed rest of those who don't presume to be God. Honor your body by recognizing its limitations—or the next stage of the journey will be too much. Tom eventually figured out a rhythm that worked. But as June slipped into July and August, and an even busier fall loomed ahead for me, I attempted to bury the precariousness of my situation with the smiling, busy-young-mom facade that too many of us wear. "It's all good!"

But Erin wasn't buying it.

"I'm concerned," she wrote, as only a covenantal friend can do. I had given her permission to call me on my crap, after all. I had invited her into covenant, to sharing life. And on those Tuesday nights she heard in my voice the sharp exhaustion, the barely concealed impatience with my children. She observed my inability to complete basic tasks, like dishes. She saw the piles of laundry, the nearly fanatical youth ministry–related communications via email and social media, the slips in memory ("Wait, is today Tuesday?").

Tabitha, too, noticed. She heard me yell at the children; she recognized the deer-in-the-headlights look whenever the phone rang and it was someone from church. Her hugs were wordless; she poured me cups of coffee. Those watchful, concerned brown eyes reminded me of a season at Isaiah House when the demands of graduate school had become overwhelming. A guest of ours— with whom I had become very close (and who was notoriously blunt)—looked up from her breakfast as I tore through the kitchen one morning and said, "Girl, you is a *mess*."

In moments like this, it's not only your covenantal friendships that will speak truth into your life; it's those with whom you're practicing hospitality. Somehow, by God's grace, the barriers of status can be torn down enough that a guest with whom you are sharing life can become an honest friend. In fact, this may be the best gift that hospitality gives, period. And you can either bristle at the insinuation that you are anything but a spiritual superhero or you can pause and acknowledge that, yes, you are a mess.

"This is not sustainable," Erin wrote, as only someone schooled in the honesty of her own battles with mental illness, as well as the honesty of Christian accountability, can write. And in that one message among dozens in my inbox, she called me out of the illusion that I can do all this and still have strength for the next chapter. She pointed out the second thing that was so dangerous, the thing that was, I now realize, the most dangerous of all.

Sin.

This frantic busyness, this resentment of embodiment, isn't merely an "error in overestimating our capacities," to quote theologian Stanley Hauerwas. Rather, sin "is the active and willful attempt to overreach our powers. It is the attempt to live *sui generis*, to live as if we are or can be the authors of our own stories. Our sin is, thus, a challenge to God's authorship and a denial that we are characters in the drama of the kingdom."[3] What was at stake was nothing less than my surrender to the lordship of Christ. Hauerwas again: "Just to the extent I refuse to be faithful to God's way, to live as part of God's life, my life assumes the character of rebellion."[4] Which meant that any claims I made with my mouth about this whole year of small things being about Jesus—about becoming more like him for the sake of the poor, whom he loves—were lies.

You could say that acknowledging sin, acknowledging how you are overreaching your powers in rebellion against God, is a form of self-care. It certainly isn't a call to annihilate yourself, although the gnostic, body-denying side of me would love that. If anything, it's a call to take stock of your behavior all the way down to the cellular level. God gave you this body; by what hubris do you suppose that it's yours to treat, or mistreat, as you wish? Setting yourself up for a bodily, emotional, and mental train wreck does violence to the image of God in you, to the purpose of God for you, and it helps no one, least of all those whom you claim to serve.

When new monastics describe their twelve marks or practices as "schools for conversion," they're not making some kind of money-back guarantee. Rather, they're describing what *happens*. Practice these disciplines or habits, and daily, incrementally, we turn away from the things that are not God, away from the lies that we happily let our culture feed us. We turn—convert—toward the truth; and the truth, Jesus says in John 8:32, will set us free. But this is not a freedom in which any whim goes, in which we get to treat our bodies as we please. Even ancient philosophers like Aristotle recognized otherwise, as Hauerwas points out: "Thus freedom did not reside in making choices but in being the kind of person for whom certain options simply were not open."[5]

If only this chapter could be about not eating junk food, or about giving up bacon.

I read Erin's email that day and wept. Then I closed my laptop and went on a long walk around my subdivision. I felt my heart working. I felt my *heart* working. I was getting nothing done; I was getting everything done that mattered. One small thing: a walk. But I knew it would be a long road ahead.

Back to Erin

Every being with a body will at some point struggle with something, be it physical ailments, emotional trials, or just plain aging. We shouldn't use this inevitability to avoid taking care of ourselves or of each other ("Well, to dust I return anyway!"). Our community can keep bringing up and bringing up the things we need help with: exercise, eating right, pursuing good mental and physical health. Our community, likewise, can ask if we've made too much of these things. Discern with your covenantal friends what "health" looks like to you. Ask what it looks like for them, and then choose an area to tackle. Is it your diet? How can your weekly communal meals help rather than hinder their well-being? (Hint: cut out bacon and dessert.) Is it your emotional well-being? How can those friends be better listeners for you?

And how can you better advocate for your own health? For me, beyond medicine, I have to constantly look at my calendar and make the time for rest and solitude. For others, time with other people is crucial for checking in and asking for prayer. What's the practice that makes you feel well? Now share that with someone. We hold pretty much no part of our lives as private. The moral of the story is group discernment, especially over the areas of our lives that intersect. Our health is one we share. How are you taking care of your body, and how are you helping others take care of theirs?

•••••

Another truth-telling moment: Sarah and I planned out the year of small things with this vague sense that self-care was important, but we didn't know exactly where it fit. I joked that "social justice is hard, so it should go last." We spent most of June, frankly, ambivalent about self-care. "Why are we doing this again?" Tom would ask. We'd reply that it was all about reminding ourselves that we need rest. "But wasn't that what we did in January when we focused on how we spend our time?" Dave would ask. And then we'd get distracted by a small child spilling a glass of water and never really settle our general unease. "It just sounds kind of like it doesn't fit."

Only now that the year is almost complete do we see the wisdom of practicing self-care as a prequel to social justice. As would-be new monastics, we want to dive right in to the justice and reconciliation stuff; that's why a lot of us are compelled by new monasticism in the first place. But it's in stopping and reminding ourselves of our finiteness that we're really able to simply be there—as a witness, as a servant of God, as neighbors—wherever social justice is concerned. Which is everywhere, and also right here in front of us.

When I was younger, one of my uncles would read this Sesame Street book to me—*There's a Monster at the End of This Book*—that my brothers and I would just giggle over (my uncle Karl does a great Grover voice). Grover sees the title and constructs these elaborate but ridiculous attempts not to let us turn the next page because he's afraid of the monster at the end. He ties ropes and builds a brick wall to deter us from turning the page (spoiler alert: Grover is the monster at the end of the book). Karl would lie back on the floor and scream, "You turned the page!" Karl's a riot.

In a way, I'm tying ropes here on the pages and asking you to stop before you turn the page. Consider what's in the next chapter. There could be a monster at the end of this book, and it is the illusion that now that we've done all this heart work, God will unleash us and we'll save—I don't know, our city, struggling schools, the homeless, the planet, whales—something!

Remember, you are finite. I, Erin, am building a brick wall so you cannot turn the page until you realize this.

We do well to stand firm in our convictions that we're finite people. We will, if we have hearts beating in our chests and if we hear the crescendo of God's work in our lives, be tempted to do more than we can sustain. Racial segregation in our churches? Let's hold a forum. Broken schools? Let's volunteer once a week. The ozone layer? Let's bike everywhere. Plant nothing but kale in our front yard—feed the homeless and cut out mowing at the same time! Take the kids to school, and be a gracious wife, friend, daughter, and church staff member. And babysit someone's child so she can go to work, and give someone a ride. And preach, write, run, and rest. I'm taking the yellow pill, remember? I'm all good!

No. Stop.

This self-care conversation is pure fluff if you don't understand this one crucial point: we're not about to "tackle" any problem. None of our work will "solve" any crisis.

Stop.

You are finite. Take care of yourself. Eat this bread. Celebrate God's victory through communion with your church. Rest. Only then can we be there as peers, witnesses, brothers and sisters in Christ.

You with us?

Okay then, let's go. Turn the page.

~~~~~ *Questions for Reflection and Discussion* ~~~~~~

1. In what ways have you struggled with matters of the body (physical, mental, emotional)? Do you feel you could share your story within your covenantal friendships?
2. If you've struggled with taking care of yourself (mental, physical, emotional, vocational), in what ways can someone hold you accountable?
3. How do you see radical faith and the marks of new monasticism competing against the value of taking care of yourself? How do you see the marks of new monasticism complementing self-care?

~~~~~ *For Further Reading* ~~~~~~~

Greene-McCreight, Kathryn. *Darkness Is My Only Companion: A Christian Response to Mental Illness*. 2nd ed. Grand Rapids: Brazos, 2015.

Norris, Kathleen. *Acedia and Me: A Marriage, Monks, and a Writer's Life*. New York: Riverhead Books, 2010. Portions of this book were first published as *The Quotidian Mysteries: Laundry, Liturgy and "Women's Work."* Costa Mesa, CA: Paulist Press, 1998.

Nouwen, Henri. *Spiritual Direction: Wisdom for the Long Walk of Faith*. New York: HarperCollins, 2006.

Stone, Jon. *There's a Monster at the End of This Book.* New York: Golden Books, 1971. (Kidding . . . kind of.)

Walker-Barnes, Chanequa. *Too Heavy a Yoke: Black Women and the Burden of Strength*. Eugene, OR: Cascade Books, 2014.

12

just living

The best that God's people have to offer is relationships
with the poor that reflect the kind of careful, quality
attention we have in our own families.

—John M. Perkins[1]

Sarah's Story

From my kitchen window I could see him: a stranger in work
clothes, walking slowly down my suburban sidewalk. He paused
in front of our house, gazing with interest into my open garage
door. Glancing up and down the street, he ambled along another
few paces, then paused again, staring into the garage. Then he
kept on walking and turned the corner out of sight.

I was home without Tom. The boys napped down the hall. My
subdivision was eerily empty and silent, as it is most afternoons,
even in midsummer. Before my brain could engage, I strode through

the laundry room to the garage and pressed that square white button, the one that closes the garage door.

This is a confession. Whatever mental image I've conjured for you, please know that skin color is everything. Clothing, yes, and ways of moving the body. But mostly race.

Suddenly it didn't matter that I had spent the bulk of my adulthood practicing radical hospitality to strangers. It didn't matter that I had lived and worshiped and studied with people of various ethnicities, from East Africa to the American South, nor that among my closest friends from Duke are people of color whose truth telling challenges me still. It didn't even matter that many of my suburban neighbors are not white.[2] No, despite this year of small things, six years of living in suburbia had habituated in me a posture of fear, living by instinct inside a false story that sees the stranger, the other, as a threat to "the good life," however that's defined. And now I had closed my garage door, according to Matthew 25:35, on Jesus.

By the time I returned to the kitchen window, I knew what I had done. This was sin. (We warned you: chapter 11 was just the warm-up.) *I* was the monster at the end of this book. Full stop. So without allowing myself the luxury of internal debate, I stepped back through the laundry room and slammed the square button again.

Up went the garage door.

Just then the front doorbell rang.

The month of radical justice begins, this July, with one very small thing: a square white button on a wall, the sound of a doorbell. One scenario among dozens, hundreds, that continued to trouble me, a kind of mirror showing what happens when we (any of us) struggle to intentionally inhabit a counternarrative that chooses Jesus over the American Dream.

In his book *Desiring the Kingdom: Worship, Worldview, and Cultural Formation*, philosopher James K. A. Smith identifies "cultural liturgies" as those ways of being—that is, the language, narratives, and practices—that shape our imaginations in what we love and desire (indeed, what we worship).[3] Every community, not just suburbia, has its cultural liturgies that form our imaginations and desires away from the things of God. But suburbia shapes us perhaps more than any other formative culture—other than, perhaps, gated communities—to worship the idols of safety, security, and comfort.

I'm guessing I'm not the only Christian suburbanite out there who has discovered that she is on the wrong side of a parable.

You can imagine the battle that waged inside me. This wasn't a mental thing, weighing pros and cons, determining the best course of action in this particular ethical quandary. No, this was entirely visceral. Fear is primal, after all—which is why, as Scott Bader-Saye reminds us in *Following Jesus in a Culture of Fear*, fear (like sex) sells.[4] And suburban parents buy it in bulk. Every muscle in my body tensed for fight or flight, even as my brain knew exactly what was happening.

"I do not understand my own actions," the apostle Paul wrote in Romans 7:15; "for I do not do what I want, but I do the very thing I hate." This rings true now, at the end of this year of small things, more than it ever has. What rules my response in any given situation is not what my brain thinks about it but whatever bodily habits I've developed, what my imagination has schooled my body to do. Without participation in a community of faith whose language, narratives, and practices shape us in the virtues that Jesus embodies, we're not suddenly going to be "clever in a crisis."[5] As Paul says later in Romans, "Do not be conformed to this world, but be transformed by the renewing of your minds, so that you may discern what is the will of God—what is good and acceptable and perfect" (12:2). In an honest community of Christians—who are just as committed to my sanctification as I am (and often more so)—I can become habituated in a love of God that is stronger than fear, stronger than any cultural narrative that values safety, security, and comfort above all things.

When my doorbell rang that afternoon, I felt a mixture of sadness and gratitude: sadness that I had allowed my zip code to habituate me on a cellular level away from the world Jesus loves, and gratitude that God was giving me a chance to start over. I was being invited to live a different story than the one our culture tells. Here in suburbia I was being called upon to put into practice all my training in radical hospitality, all those hours of opening doors to strangers. It was these practices that I needed to engage now, or I was in danger of living a different story altogether than the story of Jesus.

I opened the door.

In front of me stood not one man but two.

Cue the third wave of fear. It was still descending down my legs and out my toes when I realized that one of the men was my neighbor, a Guatemalan evangelist who travels most of the year throughout Central and South America. I had prayed with this neighbor and his wife; we had shared meals together. Smiling, earnest, oblivious to rules regarding personal space, he grabbed my hand and introduced his friend, who clearly didn't speak English. The friend grinned shyly.

He was the man I had seen from my kitchen window.

"He is helping me with the garden," my neighbor explained, then gestured toward my garage. "The wheelbarrow—can we borrow?"

Ah. Aha. Of course.

"Yes! Yes! Anything!" I said. We walked around to the once-again-open garage, and I pointed to all our tools. I would leave the garage door open, I said; take whatever you need.

•••••

The fourth mark of new monasticism is: "lament for racial divisions within the church and our communities combined with the active pursuit of a just reconciliation." For the new monastics, justice in America is more about race relations than any other single issue. We could insert issues of the global economy and sustainability in here too, which can also be seen through the lens of race, or talk about immigration, or pollution, or education—and for the new monastics it would still boil down to race. Who is on the upper side of power? Who is making decisions without accountability? Who has the official stamp of approval to exercise physical violence, and on whom? And what role do (white) churches play in perpetuating injustice?

All of this is rightly cause for lament. And yet new monastics aren't the first to name this as a Christian practice.[6] For those in the black church, for instance, lament is not some kind of unique spiritual discipline, something you can engage or not engage. It's the material reality, the starting point of the central narrative.[7] Likewise, "active pursuit of a just reconciliation" is also tricky. Who is pursuing whom? How is "just reconciliation" defined (and by whom)? And for what purpose: to assuage white guilt or to bear witness to the kingdom of God?

In short, it's complicated. Nevertheless, new monastics are right in their assertion that to breathe in America means to participate in systems of injustice, and to follow Jesus means we no longer get to take complacent breaths. We can't simply say, "I'm not hurting anybody. I'm just living, okay?" Christians cannot *just live*; rather, Christians must seek to *live justly*.

In order to combat the lies into which we are habituated—to find ourselves back on the right side of the parables—we need a conversion. We need a process for becoming more like Jesus. And that process begins with lament.

I lamented that day at my kitchen window. I lamented all summer as protests over police brutality erupted into violence around the country.[8] I grieved that Boko Haram or Al Shabaab could snuff out African lives en masse with barely a blip of mention in American social media. And when a young white man named Dylann Roof gunned down nine black Christians at Emanuel African Methodist Episcopal Church in downtown Charleston, South

Carolina, I put my face on the parsonage carpet and pounded the floor.

This was lament: not merely the grief but the anger too. This was the "How long, O Lord?" of the psalms and the prophets. Couldn't God flex some muscles now? I grieved for our black congregation back in Durham—where gracious men and women had greeted us every Sunday morning, despite the long history of whites entering black spaces for the purposes of reasserting white power. But this lament wasn't from the underside of the story; I had no business doing anything but listening to those who have borne the brunt of violence and oppression. This was lament for my own complicity, that my sons would be raised by a woman who, one sunny summer day, closed the door on a person of color.

I'm still lamenting. In some ways, my one small practice this month could begin and end there, with grief that "the color line"—in my city, in my state, in our churches—runs right through my white suburban heart. But the fourth mark of new monasticism does not end with simply feeling badly; it ends with the *pursuit* of a "just reconciliation." Not simply posting corrections to false ideas circling on the internet; not just signing online petitions or mentioning all these things as prayer requests ("slacktivism," some call it). But pursuit. Going after something. Chasing it down.

Once again, here is where my church and my circle of covenantal friends teach me. Here is where the practices of my community can draw me closer to the One (as Ps. 34:18 promises) who draws near to the brokenhearted.

Erin's Story

One July morning toward the end of this year of small things, Sycamore Creek Church's staff walked across the street to meet some neighbors. As we pushed through the brown metal doors of Mt. Hope STEAM School, our eyes adjusted to the interior hallway, our ears to the sound of a maintenance employee waxing floors in the public middle school, currently on summer break.

Mt. Hope had existed for decades as an elementary school nestled into the Sycamore Park residential neighborhood. Now it houses Lansing's two-year-old public magnet school that focuses on science, technology, engineering, art, and math. The principal's energy was palpable; she's a connector of people and opportunities. She took us on a tour, and then we sat in a classroom lab to talk.

"How might we partner with you in your mission?" Tom asked her. "How can we be good neighbors? Are there things you need?"

"We need paint," the principal said, gesturing toward chipping paint near the ceiling. "We need to feel like something new is happening here."

"We can make that happen," Tom said.

"And we need relationships—mentors, volunteers," she said. "People's time is really valuable."

It's one thing to organize volunteers to paint some hallways—which our church, along with the Sycamore Park Neighborhood Association, did with much success a few months later. It's more intimidating to think that we might have some role to play in students' lives, week after week, year after year. Yet God was here, and it was time to get in on what God was already doing.

Now that we were planted in this soil, becoming grafted into this community, we couldn't *just live* here. We couldn't simply show up on Sundays, taking over the nearby business parking lots for an hour or two and drawing from the city's power grid. We couldn't simply move into the area but then send our children to suburban schools. Rather, the principal's request reminded us that we needed to *live justly*. Real people inhabit America's urban centers, not caricatures, not statistics. Real children walk the halls of the middle school across the street. And while these students have incredible strengths—intelligence, good humor, perseverance—they also have needs.

So the key question animating this final month in the year of small things is, how can we as a worshiping body leverage our resources and our access to power on behalf of those who struggle? It's a justice question; it's about righting wrongs. And we're pretty sure God cares about righting wrongs. But it's also a relationship question. I can't contribute to change in God's city if I don't know the people God has planted here.

The first step, our pastor knew, is to walk across the street and shake a neighbor's hand. The second step, as Tom demonstrated, is not to insert our own ideas about what our neighbor needs; rather, we ask, how can we be good neighbors to you? The third step is to follow through on what we hear. Paint some school hallways? Absolutely. (We had such an amazing turnout that we painted the gym too, for good measure.) Build ongoing relationships with children? A bit trickier.

Dave and I began to sense it was time for Team Wasinger to step up to the plate.

•••••

A weekday morning not long after that first visit to Mt. Hope found the two of us (and Louisa) back there again, meeting with the school social worker who coordinates the mentor program.

"We want to volunteer," Dave said. I nodded; Louisa played with math cubes on the table.

"What are you interested in?" she asked. We began informally running through things we were decent at: writing, photography, videography, web design, storytelling. ("Math?" she asked. "No," we said firmly, almost before her question dissipated in the air.) Ideas poured out. We shared until we'd exhausted our daydreams; we filled out a background check and left, Louisa on Dave's shoulders.

Taking our location seriously, Dave and I sensed that we have roles to play in these schools—and I choose the phrase "we have roles" intentionally. As Christians, we are not bound by obligation, guilt, or responsibility. We see this not as an act of atonement for our own guilt but rather as a deepening of a relationship with our literal neighbors. We're compelled only by the love of Christ (see 2 Cor. 5:14). We understand how our decision to send the kids to Holt's schools negatively impacts Lansing schools—particularly its racial imbalances. Like the new monastics, we lament our complicity; we lament how our skin color makes the complicity even more complex. But also, like the new monastics, we want to combine lament with "the active pursuit of a just reconciliation." Our posture is humility, not pride. Our time and our talents are from God; we cannot boast about this. We are not done talking about these things, not done working toward reconciliation—which for us begins with the simple, not-so-simple practice of building relationships.

So here's what this looks like on the ground: On one of the first chilly fall days, I walked into the old foyer of Mt. Hope—then a creamy white and dark hardwood ordeal; our volunteers hadn't yet painted a colorful mural above the wainscoting.

"Erin! Hi. We're just getting in from recess," the school social worker said, brushing drizzle from her hair. Dozens of students darted around her, their cheeks red from the wind and their sneakers squeaking on the tile.

I waved and smiled, signed in, grabbed a green "volunteer" sticker. As students hung up coats in lockers, I waited in the hallway. The orange stone floor shone under a sixth grader's feet as he stooped to drink from a much shorter water fountain. The Empire had built this school with craftsmanship; the thick wood molding, the beautiful woodworking in the foyer, and the colorful slabs of stone imparted an impression of care, investment. But peeling paint hinted at the Empire's retreat.

"Oh, here she is," the social worker said, gesturing my way as the sixth-grade teacher held out her hand to me. "This is Erin, our resident storyteller." Neither woman, I think, caught the look of surprise on my face at this unexpected label, given so breezily on this, my first visit. Go with it, I thought, still smiling.

Within a few moments, I was in the classroom leading a group storytelling game—"Fortunately, Unfortunately"—and fumbling through everyone's names. This is simple stuff. I love to write, and these kids love to tell stories. Every other week I prepare a short activity, then we write and retell our stories. I'm there about an hour, but what happens during that time is a highlight of my Friday afternoons. Each time, I see God at work.

In one instance, I asked the kids to write a story about their past—real or imagined. "You can tell me about the time you rode a pterodactyl to school, even," I said. Pencils moved on everyone's papers, except one. One boy was agitated, rocking and saying he couldn't talk about his past; it was too painful.

A girl next to me, her long black hair and dark-rimmed glasses somehow a mash-up of maturity and innocence, said, "Can I go talk to him?" I nodded. She knelt next to him, putting her hand on his arm. "Hey, it's okay. Remember how much you like dragons? Can you write a story with a dragon in it?" Watching the compassion she had for her classmate was the only story I remember from that afternoon. *There*, I thought. God's here.

•••••

Being there. This is one miniscule way we can take part in the restoration of public schools that doesn't require an act of Congress. Who knows how our relationship with Mt. Hope will impact our relationship with the Lansing school district? What I do know: I have to be there to find out. Certainly, we are not under the illusion that merely being a storyteller or painting a hallway will "fix" public education—or our hearts. But we hope our presence speaks to the determination we have to build meaningful relationships—and to let those relationships change our family and our church in ways we can't control or predict.

We hope it speaks to our determination to let these relationships be a catalyst for understanding how best to advocate for systemic change too. Because, as Ronald Sider asserts in *Just*

Politics, we cannot stop on the individual level. We can pray for relationships to shape our understanding, but we can also help others to have a voice in politics by being present ourselves: in school boards, city councils, parent-teacher associations, state legislatures, public forums, social media, hearings, news outlets, and more.[9]

But I caution two things. First, we can't forget that it is not we who will bring change; it's Jesus. God is already at work here. We could easily become discouraged by the scope of the injustice. We can't disengage when our efforts seem so small. But, second, we mustn't engage blindly. How can we offer assistance without knowing the consequences to our brothers and sisters, our neighbors and friends? Knowing starts with listening, which leads to understanding—which is, essentially, the Christian practice of discernment. Yes, we're back to that again.

Back to Sarah

Not long after the year of small things drew to a close, Dave, Erin, and I found ourselves sitting, once again, around a table. It was a Tuesday in late fall—at midday, not dinnertime. And we weren't at the parsonage but seated at a conference table in the computer room of a refugee resettlement agency in downtown Lansing. At the table sat the agency's director, our friend Emily from church, and Pastor Rob Cook from Mt. Hope United Methodist Church, a neighboring urban congregation around the corner from Sycamore Creek Church.

Outside that room, beyond the walls of that building, scattered by the thousands around our city, were refugee "newcomers" from all over the world—many of them from Africa. Michigan is one of the top states for refugee resettlement in the country, with Lansing among the list of "Welcoming Cities."[10] Rob's church was becoming a magnet for these families, especially now that its new associate pastor, Eric Mulanda Nduwa, happened to be

Congolese (as well as a former soccer star in his home country). We were intrigued. Now that SCC had its own building, it made sense to jump in on what God was already doing with our nearest denominational neighbors. This, combined with Erin and Dave's background in refugee resettlement, led to what seemed like an obvious series of Tuesday lunch conversations, over the course of several weeks, with agencies, organizations, and clergy around the city.

But it was more than that. Mere weeks before this, our own state leaders had effectively told the world, "You know that little refugee, the Syrian toddler whose body washed up on the beach in Turkey? Kids like that aren't welcome here."

Warning: don't say things like that to practitioners of radical Christian hospitality.

Don't say that to moms of young children who have just spent a year teaching their kids to befriend Jesus in the poor, the outcast, the one with his "back against the wall."[11]

Don't say that to those who lament their own complicity within systems of injustice.

Tell us to shut the door on a stranger, and you'll watch us fight the fear that resides even in our own bodies to keep that door open.

"When you consider all the puzzle pieces that go into resettling refugees in Lansing," we asked the director after she shared the vision and work of her agency, "when you think of all the programs involved, is there anything missing?"

She thought for a moment. "Probably it's the one-on-one relationships," she said. "It's the local families connecting with newcomers in an ongoing way."

I looked across the table at Erin, who was already looking at me. "Churches can do that," we said. "This fits."

•••••

The summer of lament, which brought this year of small things to a close, sent us from the parsonage table out into our city. And this is as it should be. We can't stay only at that table, in the safe circle of our covenantal friendships. We can't always expect the poor to come to us, even though sharing life with the stranger through the Christian practice of hospitality is vital to all our conversions. We can't forever be lamenting, as if our hands are otherwise tied by accidents of race or class or zip code. We must leave our homes, close our laptops, walk the streets of our cities, look and listen—discern—where the Spirit of God is calling.

For the Arthurs and the Wasingers, our discernment during this month led us to some fairly simple practices: volunteer in an urban school every other Friday; paint its hallways; network with those involved in refugee resettlement; start a Tuesday lunch discussion group on welcoming refugees—which we anticipate will lead to ongoing friendships with newcomer families.[12] Small things, hardly heroic. There are many, many other things we could be doing.[13] But, as Stanley Hauerwas says, "I do not have to think about doing everything or nothing; I do not have to begin by trying to 'solve' the real problem. Instead I can take the time to do one thing that might help lead myself and others to God's peace."[14] *Finitude*, we remind ourselves; the job of savior has already been taken.

So how about you?

Begin with discernment. Become educated about the struggles your city faces; God speaks in those details. Gather your covenantal group to do the holy work of lamenting—of acknowledging your complicity in injustice but confidently waiting for God to act. Listen humbly to those with whom you are practicing hospitality; what are *their* dreams for your city? Then begin to imagine who is missing from the table. Who can help you better understand what's going on? Who is directly impacted? Who is already working toward reconciliation or justice—whom can you join? Pray for clarity. Wait. Pray some more.

One last word of caution before we close this chapter: When we begin to dream about our cities, we must not fool ourselves into thinking that "acts of kindness" suffice. Being with our neighbors isn't a way we assuage our guilt. "Somehow we have to disconnect what and how we give from our need to feel good about ourselves," Christian community development activist John Perkins asserts.[15] *Somehow*, Perkins cautions: this is the nuance that speaks to God's work in this process. Yes, as all year we've trained our minds to be still and watch for the Holy Spirit's movement in our lives, so too are we guided in areas of social justice.

Your covenantal group at this point has been praying for you since that first dinner. These friends know how you spend your money and your Sabbaths; they understand how many children, commitments, and Lego bins you have. The same folks have asked you tough questions about church, your most intimate relationships, and your own health. Listen to them urgently; their voices might be used by God to tell you if the way you're serving others springs from the love of Christ—or from something else.

Is this year of small things about Jesus or me?

Is this about Jesus or you?

~~~~~~ *Questions for Reflection and Discussion* ~~~~~~

1. What does racial reconciliation look like in your community? What are its fruits?

2. In what ways does fear dictate your actions?

3. Do you feel drawn to a particular cause or group of people? What fuels your desire to help? What hinders you from becoming involved?

4. How does one disconnect the urge to help from the desire to feel good about oneself? How do you know when you're acting out of love for Christ or in your own self-interest?

~~~~~~ **For Further Reading** ~~~~~~~~~~~~~~~~~~~~~~~~~

Bader-Saye, Scott. *Following Jesus in a Culture of Fear*. Grand Rapids: Brazos, 2007.

Marsh, Charles, and John M. Perkins. *Welcoming Justice: God's Movement toward Beloved Community*. Downers Grove, IL: InterVarsity, 2009.

Perkins, John M. *Beyond Charity: The Call to Christian Community Development*. Grand Rapids: Baker, 1993.

Wallis, Jim. *America's Original Sin: Racism, White Privilege, and the Bridge to a New America*. Grand Rapids: Brazos, 2016.

Wilson-Hartgrove, Jonathan. *Free to Be Bound: Church beyond the Color Line*. Colorado Springs: NavPress, 2008.

closing thoughts

We began this book with a snapshot of me (Sarah) on a sunny fall day washing a car in my suburban driveway. As I said before, it was not my car. And I promised I'd explain how that story unfolded, how all those months in this year of small things came together for me in one iconic moment. So here it is.

In midsummer Tom and I had sold the Petoskey house. We had gone up north in May to work on the place and reconnect with our renter, who had not been in touch with us for months, but we found when we arrived that he had moved out, leaving only a brief, congenial note but no forwarding address. The empty house felt like a blow; Jesus was gone, and I didn't even get to say good-bye. But we steadily got through the work that needed doing, put the house on the market, and sold it within three weeks. We had been hoping to make what we owed on it and perhaps a little more. What we didn't expect was a seller's market and a net windfall of over thirty thousand dollars (we're not kidding about financial transparency).

Never in all our years of adulting had we seen that many digits in our bank account.

What does a typical American do with thirty thousand extra dollars? I can hazard a guess. I know what *I* would do: I'd take an overseas trip, replace my wardrobe, buy original editions of beloved books, and make a down payment on a VW camper van. I'm sure you have your own list. But after practicing the marks of radical faith in covenantal friendship with folks who were keeping us accountable, we knew we needed to put our personal lists aside. We knew we needed to prioritize the things God cares about, the things that form us—our family, our church, our community— more into the image of Jesus.

The first step? Tithe to our church's capital campaign so our building can continue to serve the neighborhood. The next step: pay off debt. All of it. Both cars, outstanding bills from work on the Petoskey house, everything. As of this writing, we are now officially debt-free. Third step: rebuild our family's depleted emergency fund. Fourth: create a long-term emergency fund so that each new circumstance doesn't bind us in more debt, unable to help others. Finally, we gave ourselves some mad money to replace our living room futon—which we had purchased seven years ago from another grad student—with a real grown-up couch.

"This is *really* nice," I said one date night at a furniture store before dinner. I leaned back into the couch's black leather, running my hands along its casual, extra-wide stitching. Tom sat adjacent from me on a matching overstuffed armchair, his feet propped up on an ottoman. We settled in, reveling in this chance to celebrate. We had used most of what we had made on what we hoped were wise, generous practices; now, like the partygoers in the parables, we got to kill the fatted calf—so to speak.

"This is really nice too," Tom said, inspecting the chair. We looked at price tags. We hadn't planned on the chair—it was an added luxury that would bump up our total significantly. But, wow, a matching set. We could get into this celebration stuff.

"We need to think about this," Tom said to the salesperson who was taking notes. "We'll be back."

Over dinner we continued talking. We weighed pros and cons, discussed other items we'd like to buy—especially now that we had successfully hosted not one but *two* garage sales in our war against "stuff." Finally, I said out loud what needed saying: "What would Erin and Dave think about all this? And also, what about Grace's car?"

This is discernment; this is where a year of radical faith takes you. When facing a decision, the first people you think of are those who will lovingly tell you the truth—people who will make you do the hard thing for Jesus. The other people you think of are those in your community who have significant needs, whose burdens have now become your burdens. Our friend Grace (not her real name) needed a car. She was a single mom on public assistance who struggled to get her children to doctor's appointments, much less to church. And yet, week after week, month after month, she served countless hours in our church's ministries. And week after week, her requests would show up in the email that went out to the prayer team: "Please, God, I need a car."

"I keep thinking about that too," Tom said.

There was only a moment's pause before he opened his smartphone as I said, "What's our budget? Sixteen hundred? What can we get her for that?"

A few hours later we were test-driving a vehicle we found on Craigslist. I messaged Erin: "You'll never believe what's happening." She messaged back, raving with excitement.

A few days later, the car was Grace's.

That sunny fall day, it was her car I was washing in my driveway when that other vehicle drove by, the one with the camera documenting the street view. Our new couch and ottoman had not yet been delivered; there would be no matching chair. But in that moment I knew: Whatever else that vehicle recorded—a suburban woman washing a suburban car in front of her suburban house—it also documented an ongoing conversion. A year of small things, twelve months of small but radical practices, all adding up to a life being transformed, slowly over time, by the grace of a patient, generous God.

●●●●●

So where does this experiment leave us, the Arthurs and the Wasingers?

We still meet for dinner every week, whenever possible. We're on year two of radical faith. We still ask how nightly prayer and date nights are going, about whether we're keeping the Sabbath. We discuss where we see God at work in all those Mt. Hopes—the school and our sister church—and how we might jump in. Out of respect for my heart and the "pigness of the pig," bacon is no longer a communal staple. Tabitha rushes through the kitchen between jobs, greeting everyone with a blessing. Just last week we opened our screens again to review all those squares and rectangles, to consider the ways home ownership and home divestment have recalibrated how we see God using our finances. The Christmas letter went out again; this year the church's Christmas Eve offering brought in more than $16,000.

And still, every week, we close with the prayer circle. Our children gather with us around the flameless candle; we share what made us happy this week, what made us sad. We pray the Our Father and sing "Go Now in Peace."

We're pretty sure we're not changing the world. But we're letting God change us, which in turn points us toward the change already happening in our church and city. One small thing at a time.

May this be the case for you as well.

appendix a

engaging three strands
of radical christianity

In our reading and conversations for this project, we found ourselves engaging roughly three strands or movements of radical
Christianity, mostly within Protestant evangelical American Christianity (but influenced by orders and movements within mainline
Protestantism and Catholicism as well). All these strands involve
the comfortable becoming downwardly mobile for the sake of
the afflicted, whom Christ loves. These movements go by various
names, but for the purposes of this book we'll use the following
distinctions: the new friars, the new radicals, and the new monastics. It's imperative to understand which voices we're engaging.
Let's compare.

New Friars

Scott Bessenecker's *The New Friars: The Emerging Movement
Serving the World's Poor* traces the rise of global missions to "the

least of these," staffed by downwardly mobile young Americans. Though the roots of global missions trace back to the early twentieth century, perhaps what Bessenecker finds novel is the call to long-term relocation to the poor urban centers of the developing world and living as the poor themselves do rather than in comfortable missionary compounds.

New Radicals

Megachurch pastors such as David Platt, Francis Chan, Kyle Idleman, and Eugene Cho are sucker-punching the material complacency of evangelicals. Through books like Platt's *Radical* and Idleman's *Not a Fan*, and through organizations such as Cho's One Day's Wages, evangelicals are being challenged to ditch the American Dream and pursue God's heart for the global poor, all for the sake of the gospel. Some hear echoes from a previous generation of prophets, such as Tony Campolo (*Red Letter Christians*) and Ronald Sider (*Rich Christians in an Age of Hunger*). So what's new about the new radicals is not so much the call to serve the world's poor but rather the size of the platform by which that call is being sent out—through megachurch podiums and best-selling books and social media. And the call is not just to the young (as with the new friars) but to comfortable suburbanites with children and mortgages and 401(k)s.

New Monastics

Shane Claiborne (*The Irresistible Revolution*) is one of the key spokespersons for this strand, which traces some of its roots back to the same influences that have shaped the new friars and the new radicals but takes a vastly different expression. Rather than taking a global view, the new monastics focus their attention on the "abandoned places of Empire"—that is, America's forgotten urban centers. And rather than individuals or families taking personal steps of downward mobility for the sake of the poor, new monastics form intentional Christian communities: households or networks of households that share life together (meals, prayers, chores) and in which the poor are key participants.

Among the various practices of these communities, racial reconciliation between whites and blacks is a hallmark—yet another difference between them and the new radicals. However, new monastic communities have found it hard to enlist black members in this vision of downward mobility and shared life. The practitioners of new monasticism, by and large, are mostly white; and while they have successfully engaged black churches in dialogue and offered hospitality to struggling folks of all races, their quest for reconciliation that leads to shared life and vision—church "beyond the color line," as Jonathan Wilson-Hartgrove puts it—continues to elude.

●●●●●

All three strands have influenced us in some form, with the weight of this experiment resting mostly on new monasticism. Overall, we applaud each movement in turn. But we are not without our questions or concerns.

First, we must be careful not to equate poverty with lack of faith. Too often the assumption is that the poor don't know Jesus. That may be true in some of the developing world, but that's certainly not true in countries—particularly ours—with a long history of Christianity.

Second, our call to serve alongside the poor is not a call to help the afflicted look more like the comfortable. Yes, God wants the lives of the afflicted to be less desperate, less grinding, less hopeless and helpless. But that doesn't mean he wants them to dress, act, smell, eat, or talk like middle- to upper-class Americans. In fact, he seems to be more interested in the reverse: that middle- to upper-class Americans take on the cultural marks of poverty to demonstrate that God is the God of those who, in Howard Thurman's words, "have their backs against the wall."

Third, when it comes to the lasting legacy of the new radicals in particular, what remains to be seen is whether any of this will stick. What will these megachurch pastors be doing in twenty years? Will any of them give up their platforms to follow a call into obscurity? That may not be what God has in mind for them, but we do wonder if the pace is sustainable. (What does radical retirement look like?)

Finally, a word of grace. We all need to be converted—turned toward Jesus—and it's a process that lasts a lifetime. The poor in this country can be just as focused on the trappings of the American Dream as anyone else, and we together are constantly sinking into habits or practices that win us away from Jesus. Conversion is a lifestyle. It's a process. It's a continual turning toward the things that transform our own hearts to be more like Jesus and away from those things that deform us. May we not put so much emphasis on a "movement" that we lose sight of Christ.

appendix b

hospitality covenant

Take it from folks (Sarah and Tom) who have practiced radical hospitality with strangers in various contexts for over fifteen years. shared life is far easier when you set expectations up front. Here's the nearly verbatim "covenant" we created with Tabitha, modified from one we drafted when our first guest joined us more than a dozen years ago. You'll note that it's fairly straightforward without a lot of theological jargon; it doesn't proof-text from Scripture. We hope it's a helpful jumping-off point for anyone considering sharing their home with others.

Thoughts on Life Together

1. Building community together by sharing a daily meal. (Usually dinner around 6:00 p.m. If we can't make it for dinner, we'll let one another know. We eat mostly vegetarian but do eat some meat.)
2. Sharing chores (dishes, picking up after ourselves, cooking, house laundry, yard work, child care, etc.).

3. Respecting appropriate boundaries (knocking on closed doors, opposite-sex visitors in living room/dining room/kitchen only, asking before we use or borrow things, keeping quiet while others are sleeping, asking about guests visiting before they visit, etc.).

4. Not abusing alcohol (if alcoholism has been a problem in the past, then alcohol should not be consumed at all), not using illegal drugs, and not smoking in the house.

5. Not having pets in the house. (Sarah is allergic to most pets.)

6. Contributing financially as able (working to find regular employment, helping with food costs, etc.).

7. Respecting and/or joining times of spiritual practices (morning prayer and evening prayer).

8. Living simply (saving resources).

9. Taking initiative to constructively resolve conflicts by talking through them peacefully (listening to one another respectfully and humbly in order to find understanding and a mutually beneficial solution; doing to others as we would have them do to us; touching base weekly and reviewing longer-term plans monthly).

Living Arrangements

1. We will provide a room and some basic furniture (bed, sheets, blankets, dresser, shelves, chair, clothes hangers, etc.).

2. We will provide basic toiletries (toilet paper, towels, etc.).

3. We will provide basic cleaning supplies (detergent, soap, etc.).

4. We will provide food for dinner (you provide breakfast, lunch, and snack food for yourself).

5. We will provide cooking supplies (dishes, glasses, pots, pans, silverware, etc.).

appendix c

the arthurs' christmas letter

No matter how good you might be at this celebration-on-a-budget thing, you still have to set boundaries for those within your extended family who have certain expectations. Gift giving may not be your "love language" (it barely registers on either my or Tom's love-language inventories), but it may be for someone else you love—and not interacting with those people in their language can be hurtful.[1] At the same time, you need boundaries.

We sent the letter below, drafted by Tom, to our extended family at the beginning of Advent during the year of small things. We were grateful not only that they lovingly responded by respecting our wishes but that many of them also expressed appreciation.

So, without further ado, here's our double-dog dare.

Dear Family,

Three different streams have come together to form the primary idea in this letter. That primary idea is that we (Tom, Sarah, Micah, and Sam) would like to celebrate Christmas differently this year and in the years to come, and we would like to invite you to consider joining us in this endeavor.

First, over the last several years we have been leading our church to celebrate Christmas differently. This has caused us to search our own souls about how we celebrate Christmas as a family. Perhaps Mike Slaughter, a United Methodist pastor in Ohio, said it best: "Christmas is not your birthday."[2] He then asks, "Do you have any presents under the Christmas tree this year to give to Jesus?" Along with many in our church, we have had to come to the realization that rarely do we ever have any presents under the tree for Jesus except for a perfunctory attendance at a Christmas Eve service (and Tom is paid to be there!).

Second, as we are now celebrating our fifth Christmas as parents, we are doing some more family soul-searching about Christmas. We find that we, like so many parents we talk to, are drowning in stuff. Stuff that is supposed to make our lives easier but that ends up creating hidden complications. Instead of owning the stuff, the stuff owns us. Just consider how much time we spend daily picking up toys! We're searching for the soul of our family amid the clutter.

Third, add to these first two streams one of Sarah's current book projects (yes, Sarah is somehow currently writing two books), The Year of Small Things. *This book is being coauthored with a friend of ours from church, Erin Wasinger. It's an attempt to reclaim some of the values of the Isaiah House (where we lived in Durham while attending Duke) and new monasticism (the "tradition" that the Isaiah House stood in) while we currently live in the suburbs. Over the next year we are picking one "small" thing each month from new monasticism and attempting to live it out more fully. One of the values we are seeking to reclaim is living simply when it comes to the accumulation of stuff.*

You can see how these three streams come together in a powerful way during the month of December and in our celebration of Christmas. So we would like to make two proposals and invite you to consider joining us.

First, beginning with this Christmas, we'd like to ask that whatever you would spend on Tom and Sarah, you would instead give that amount to our church's Christmas offering. This year, our Christmas offering will be used to support our medical missions in Nicaragua, the United Methodist Church's Imagine No Malaria campaign to eradicate malaria (*www.imaginenomalaria.org*), and local emergency needs (rent, utilities, food, etc.) of Lansing families. We believe these are gifts that together we can put under the tree for Jesus.

Second, we would like to ask you to limit gifts for Micah and Sam to one gift each at Christmas (feel free to go hog wild at their birthdays). If they receive one gift each from everyone in our family, they will each receive somewhere between eight and ten gifts! That really is plenty, isn't it? We will then begin asking them to give away one toy for every new toy they receive.

Meanwhile, our gifts to you will be things that we make together, especially with the boys: art projects, homemade canned goods, copies of Sarah's books, and so on. This reflects our desire to be creators rather than consumers.

That's it. Three streams and two proposals. Pretty easy, right? Well, it's always cleaner on paper than in reality, and we're sure that there are things we haven't thought about and complications that will arise. We aren't trying to make this a new law, and there is plenty of mercy and grace in our intentions. The last thing we want to do is to become judgmental about any of this. We're wanting to let you know where we're at. You may be in a very different place, and we're open to ongoing conversation about it all.

May we experience God's blessing this Christmas season in our times together and our gifts to one another and to Jesus.

Love,
Tom and Sarah

P.S. If you were planning to give a million dollars to Micah's or Sam's education funds, then everything we have said above is null and void. (Just kidding . . . sorta.)

Notes

Introduction

1. Thomas Merton, trans., *The Wisdom of the Desert: Sayings from the Desert Fathers of the Fourth Century* (Boston: Shambhala, 1960), 167.

2. See our exploration and critiques of three different contemporary strands of American Christian "radicals" in appendix A.

3. The Rutba House, *School(s) for Conversion. 12 Marks of a New Monasticism* (Eugene, OR: Cascade Books, 2005), xii–xiii.

4. Matthew Lee Anderson, "Here Come the Radicals," *Christianity Today*, March 2013, 22.

5. A phrase Howard Thurman uses throughout his timeless *Jesus and the Disinherited* (1949; repr., Boston: Beacon, 1996).

Chapter 1 Covenantal Friendship

1. As Stanley Hauerwas writes in *The Peaceable Kingdom: A Primer in Christian Ethics* (Notre Dame, IN: University of Notre Dame Press, 1983), generally in life, most of us "expand the circle of our friends very carefully because we intuitively know that we must not welcome any into our lives who might raise questions that challenge our illusions. Our 'circle of friends' in fact becomes a conspiracy of intimacy to protect each of our illusions" (141).

2. In *Discernment: Reading the Signs of Daily Life* (New York: HarperOne, 2015), Henri Nouwen calls the act of listening to the Spirit's movement a key part of our perpetual growth (see p. 8). Practicing it in community can strengthen the listening we do individually through Bible study, in prayer, and in nature.

3. Jon Stock, Tim Otto, and Jonathan Wilson-Hartgrove, *Inhabiting the Church: Biblical Wisdom for a New Monasticism* (Eugene, OR: Cascade Books, 2007), 26.

4. Dietrich Bonhoeffer, *Life Together* (San Francisco: HarperSanFrancisco, 1954), 26.

Chapter 2 Hospitality beyond Martha Stewart

1. With the exception of folks who practice foster parenting and/or adoption. Also, throughout his years at Wheaton College, Tom had worshiped regularly at Jesus People USA on the north side of Chicago, so he had witnessed radical hospitality on a large-scale communal level. But we hadn't seen hospitality practiced primarily alongside adults within single-family households.

2. Tom reminded me that we tithed the income from that room to our church's capital campaign for the first year. At the time we weren't able to give more money to the church, but we realized our new house had almost ten (mostly small) rooms: what if we tithed one of them?

3. One of the things we (the Arthurs) shared at that meal was the covenant we had made with Tabitha when she moved in. We encouraged the others to create similar covenants so that mutual expectations are clear up front and hospitality over time doesn't become an area of deep bitterness and stress. We've included the covenant in appendix B.

4. For instance, Jesus asserts in places such as Mark 14:7 and John 12:8 that the poor will always be with the disciples; the first deacons, including Stephen, were set apart by the apostles to oversee the care of the community's widows (see Acts 6:1–6); the disciples took up a collection for the relief of believers affected by famine (see Acts 11:27–30); and in 1 Corinthians 16:1–3 the apostle Paul gave instructions for a special "collection for the saints."

Chapter 3 Radical Finances

1. Jonathan Wilson-Hartgrove, *God's Economy: Redefining the Health and Wealth Gospel* (Grand Rapids: Zondervan, 2009), 147.

2. We got this idea from the book *Financial Parenting* by Larry Burkett (Colorado Springs: Chariot Victor, 1996).

3. We appreciate the practical wisdom of Ronald J. Sider's work, particularly *Rich Christians in an Age of Hunger*, 5th ed. (Nashville: Thomas Nelson, 2005), where the idea of a graduated tithe is explained (see pp. 187–94). In short, giving increases as income increases.

4. To clarify, our grocery budget includes toiletries, diapers, household supplies, and even some medicine—as does the Wasingers'—but it's mostly food.

5. In a conversation with Tony Campolo in *Red Letter Revolution: What If Jesus Really Meant What He Said?* (Nashville: Thomas Nelson, 2012), Claiborne makes a case against Christians saving for retirement on the grounds that it goes

against a radical abandon to God's providence (see pp. 18–19). Full disclosure: Dave's retirement account is still accruing.

6. Richard Foster, *Money, Sex and Power: The Challenge of the Disciplined Life* (New York: HarperCollins, 1985), 30. In this book Foster offers a rebuke to Ramsey's concept of money as a "tool" that Christians should use to do good. Foster writes that Jesus gave "mammon" a persona (see Matt. 6:24), describing it as something with power and force (see p. 52). We can't pretend not to be influenced by the allure of having more.

Chapter 4 Reclaiming Spiritual Habits

1. Nathan Foster, *The Making of an Ordinary Saint: My Journey from Frustration to Joy with the Spiritual Disciplines* (Grand Rapids: Baker Books, 2014), 66.

2. Dietrich Bonhoeffer, *Life Together* (San Francisco: HarperSanFrancisco, 1954), 73.

3. From Psalm 134 in Daily Devotions for Individuals and Families, *Book of Common Prayer* (New York: Church Hymnal Corporation, 2007), http://www.bcponline.org/.

4. Lauren F. Winner, *Still: Notes from a Mid-faith Crisis* (New York: HarperOne, 2012), 190.

5. Benedicta Ward, trans., *The Desert Fathers: Sayings of the Early Christian Monks* (New York: Penguin, 2003), 130.

6. Saint Ignatius Loyola's prayers reflected on the day: Where did one encounter God? Where did one feel far from God? The *examen* typically has five elements, but this emphasis on recounting the day is central. See "Ignatian Spirituality: The Daily Examen," accessed January 15, 2016, http://jesuits.org/spirituality?PAGE=DTN-20130520125910.

7. Shane Claiborne, Jonathan Wilson-Hartgrove, and Enuma Okoro, *Common Prayer: A Liturgy for Ordinary Radicals* (Grand Rapids: Zondervan, 2010).

8. Bonhoeffer, *Life Together*, 47.

Chapter 5 Stuff

1. Richard Foster, *The Celebration of Discipline*, in *Treasury of Christian Discipline*, rev. ed. (San Francisco: HarperCollins, 1988), 191.

2. I jest, but Sarah makes me point out that it's because the Christmas holiday wasn't put on the calendar until centuries after Paul's death. Sarah loves to ruin a good joke with her seminary degree.

3. The familiar American Christmas really took off as Civil War–weary families were nostalgic for peace. Gift giving increased in popularity among family and friends and then in the form of small gifts to charity out of "Christian duty." See Penne Restad, "Christmas in 19th Century America," *History Today* 45, no. 12 (December 1995), http://www.historytoday.com/penne-restad/christmas-19th-century-america. This history provides new monastics their strongest argument

against a mere "season" of giving: their practices make economic sharing neither purely missional nor a once-a-year affair.

4. See Exod. 22:22; Jer. 7:6; Zech. 7:10; James 1:27; and numerous other places in Scripture.

Chapter 6 Holy Time

1. Walter Brueggemann, *Sabbath as Resistance: Saying No to the Culture of Now* (Louisville: Westminster John Knox, 2014), 27.

2. David Robinson, *The Busy Family's Guide to Spirituality: Practical Lessons for Modern Living from the Monastic Tradition* (New York: Crossroad, 2009), 10.

3. Brueggemann, *Sabbath as Resistance*, 30–31.

4. Many thanks to my ethics professor, Amy Laura Hall of Duke Divinity School, for this important reminder. I first heard her say this to a group of high school students and faculty at the Duke Youth Academy for Christian Formation in 2006.

5. Brueggemann, *Sabbath as Resistance*, 23.

6. Ibid., 29.

7. The Israelite slaves ask permission to leave for a short time to worship their God. Pharaoh refuses, calling the slaves lazy. He retaliates by ordering the Israelites to start collecting their own straw while still meeting the same quota of bricks (see Exod. 5). God rescues the Israelites from this slavery but doesn't let them forget where they came from. Throughout Deuteronomy, he says again and again, "Remember, you were slaves." This reminder is a prompt: God offers a better alternative to the "no straw, more bricks" model. Brueggemann writes that when we fail to rest, we are forgetting this Exodus narrative (*Sabbath as Resistance*, 20–34).

Chapter 7 Vows

1. Ronald J. Sider, *The Scandal of the Evangelical Conscience* (Grand Rapids: Baker Books, 2005), 125.

2. Francis and Lisa Chan, *You and Me Forever: Marriage in Light of Eternity* (San Francisco: Claire Love Publishing, 2014), 113.

3. Tim Otto, *Oriented to Faith: Transforming the Conflict over Gay Relationships* (Eugene, OR: Cascade Books, 2014), 13.

4. Ibid., 17.

5. This is a review of Rachmaninoff's first work: "If there were a conservatory in Hell, and if one of its talented students was to compose a symphony based on the story of the Seven Plagues of Egypt, and if he had written one similar to Rachmaninoff's, he would have brilliantly accomplished his task and would have delighted the inhabitants of Hell" (Lansing Symphony Orchestra program notes, 2015–2016, accessed October 16, 2015, http://www.lansingsymphony.org/Portals/0/docs/Program%20Notes%20-%20MW2%20Together.pdf).

Chapter 8 Planted in the Church

1. Paul Sparks, Tim Soerens, and Dwight J. Friesen, *The New Parish: How Neighborhood Churches Are Transforming Mission, Discipleship and Community* (Downers Grove, IL: InterVarsity, 2014), 24.

2. "Crime in America 2015: Top 10 Most Dangerous Cities under 200,000," accessed January 19, 2016, http://lawstreetmedia.com/crime-america-2015-top -10-dangerous-cities-200000/.

3. "Your parish is a microcosm that helps bring many cause-and-effect relationships back together again. Being in collaborative relationships in real life (where you live, work and play) awakens you to the effects of your actions both on people and on the place itself. It creates a context where your church can see whether its faith is more than just talk. The local place becomes the testing ground, revealing whether you have learned to love each other and the larger community around you. In essence, the parish is a dare to your faith" (Sparks, Soerens, and Friesen, *New Parish*, 24).

4. When Pastor Barb Flory and her team founded Sycamore Creek Church, they chose the name by asking people who didn't attend church which name would be more approachable. Barb was angling for something like "Hope" or "Faith," but they chose the reference to a creek that runs through parts of Lansing. Fifteen years later, we're literally right down the street from Sycamore Creek.

5. The median income in Michigan's capital city is about $12,000 less than the statewide average; nearly 30 percent of Lansing's residents live below the poverty level, compared to about 17 percent across the state (United States Census Bureau, "QuickFacts: Lansing City, Michigan," accessed September 18, 2015, http://quickfacts.census.gov/qfd/states/26/2646000.html).

6. For quick context, 39 percent of children in the district live in poverty (nationwide, it's about 22.5 percent). Only about 14 percent of adults who live within the district's boundaries have bachelor's degrees or higher—nationally, districts reported a 28.5 percent average (Lansing School District, "Choice Helps Individuals Learn and Develop," accessed September 22, 2015, http://www2.ed .gov/programs/magnet/2013/lansingapp.pdf).

7. Eric O. Jacobsen's *Sidewalks in the Kingdom: New Urbanism and the Christian Faith* (Grand Rapids: Brazos, 2003) is a beautiful argument for sharing life with others in cities, especially in public spaces such as sidewalks and parks. What makes suburbia an often lonely place is the lack of sidewalks and destination green spaces. Our Lansing neighborhood features an urban walking/biking trail, a large metropark, and well-kept sidewalks, which encourages activity and critical mass where we live.

8. Stanley Hauerwas, *The Peaceable Kingdom: A Primer in Christian Ethics* (Notre Dame, IN: University of Notre Dame Press, 1983), xiv.

Chapter 9 Kid Monasticism

1. Hannah Whitall Smith, *The Christian's Secret of a Happy Life* (New York: Revell, 1888), 34.

2. Anne Lamott, *Bird by Bird: Some Instructions on Writing and Life* (New York: Anchor Books, 1994), 170.

3. Nine out of ten third graders in some schools failed state-issued tests for reading and math. While we as a family don't put much weight on standardized tests, the low scores certainly mar the district's reputation in the general population (Lansing School District, "Choice Helps Individuals Learn and Develop," accessed January 14, 2016, http://www2.ed.gov/programs/magnet/2013/lansing app.pdf).

4. For perspective, consider that the 2013 makeup of the city itself was 72 percent white to 28 percent minority. The district struggles with what it calls "black student isolation" (ibid.).

5. MI School Data, "Free and Reduced Lunch Counts," accessed September 27, 2016, https://www.mischooldata.org/Other/DataFiles/StudentCounts/Historical FreeAndReducedLunchCounts.aspx.

6. Sarah's good friend Elizabeth DeGaynor, director of the Master of Arts in Christian Practice program at Duke Divinity School, graciously gave us chapters to read from her unpublished dissertation, "Learning (Re)formation: An Ethnographic Study of Theological Vision and Educational Praxis at Grand Rapids Christian Schools" (Duke University, 2015). Her research into the connection between private Christian schools and issues of race is eye-opening and convicting.

7. Ronald J. Sider, *Just Politics: A Guide for Christian Engagement* (Grand Rapids: Brazos, 2012), 134.

8. Ibid., 40.

9. The Amish *rumspringa*, roughly translated as "running around," is a recognized time of adolescence in which youth are given certain leeway to explore non-Amish (or "English") practices. It culminates in either baptism or leaving the community. See "What Is Rumspringa?," accessed September 7, 2016, http://amishamerica.com/what-is-rumspringa.

10. Early Methodists gathered in "classes" (small groups within the larger "societies," or local worshiping congregations) to hold each other accountable to works of piety, works of mercy, and the Three Simple Rules (United Methodist Church, "The General Rules of the Methodist Church," accessed August 12, 2016, http://www.umc.org/what-we-believe/general-rules-of-the-methodist-church).

11. The phrase "stay in love with God" is a contemporary reframing of the original injunction to "attend upon all the ordinances of God"—in other words, practice daily spiritual habits of Bible reading, prayer, worship, and so on, because if we love God, we will seek to spend time with God. Our favorite resource for exploring these rules is *The Three Simple Rules: A Wesleyan Way of Living* by Rueben P. Job (Nashville: Abingdon, 2007).

12. Benedicta Ward, trans., *The Desert Fathers: Sayings of the Early Christian Monks* (New York: Penguin, 2003), 81.

Chapter 10 Sustaining Creation

1. For a helpful article summarizing much of what we've learned over the years, see "Could Your Lawn Be Lethal?," *Men's Health*, May 15, 2010, http ://www.menshealth.com/health/lawn-chemical-hazards. Granted, the average American may not have enough long-term exposure to cause damage to his or her nervous or reproductive systems; on principle this is more about the workers who treat the lawns all summer long and the chemical plants that dump waste into the environment. At the same time, new research into neurological diseases such as Parkinson's and Lewy Body Dementia (which members of Tom's family have faced) indicates a link between those diseases and exposure to certain pesticides (see Mayo Clinic, "Dementia," accessed January 19, 2016, http://www .mayoclinic.org/diseases-conditions/dementia/basics/causes/con-20034399).

2. For the record, my parents are also very conscientious about creation care; I just hadn't adopted these practices on my own as a young adult. Additionally, my sister, Abigail Deloria, and her husband, Phil, are artists and organic farmers at Fiddlehead Farm in northern Michigan, providing CSA (community-supported agriculture) shares to needy families through the county health department. Another one of our "small things" this year was to donate toward their community CSA shares.

3. A tour of Polyface Farm normally costs several thousand dollars because it takes Joel away from doing his real work, which is farming. Also, in one of those divine jokes that continually thwart our earnest efforts, Tom had just broken his foot, which meant that my carbon-footprint-conscious husband had to ride around one of America's most famous farms on an ATV.

4. "Individuality" is one of the principles of Polyface Farm: "Plants and animals should be provided a habitat that allows them to express their physiological distinctiveness. Respecting and honoring the pigness of the pig is a foundation for societal health" (Polyface Farm, "Polyface Guiding Principles," accessed January 19, 2016, http://www.polyfacefarms.com/principles/).

5. This happened rather abruptly, in fact. As Tom was traveling down the highway with his relatively new bike (a graduation gift) strapped on the bike rack, it suddenly flew off, bounced a few times, and landed, ruined, in the grass on the side of the road. (Thankfully, no cars were hit.) It felt at the time like the ultimate defeat: not merely "Biking may not be the best plan," but "Here, let's make sure biking is not an option, ever."

6. Earlier incarnations of this book included more stories depicting the Arthur family's discoveries about the realities of suburban poverty, particularly in Holt, which tends to have a much lower cost of housing than other Lansing suburban towns such as DeWitt, Grand Ledge, Okemos, and Williamston (something we knew instinctively but have confirmed through comparative ratings available

at www.bestplaces.net/, accessed September 16, 2016). One solid indicator of
poverty is free and reduced-price lunch counts: in Holt, 40 percent of Wilcox
Elementary School's student body qualifies for free or reduced-price lunches;
about 53 percent qualify at Sycamore Elementary. This map, based on 1980 and
2010 census data, shows how poverty has spread from cities to the suburbs in
Michigan: http://www.mlive.com/news/index.ssf/2013/07/see_how_has_poverty
_spread_in.html (Fritz Klug, "Maps: See How Poverty Has Spread to the Suburbs
in Michigan," *MLive*, July 8, 2013). The shift reflects similar national trends (see
Jennifer Medina, "Hardship Makes a New Home in the Suburbs," *New York
Times*, May 9, 2014, http://www.nytimes.com/2014/05/10/us/hardship-makes
-a-new-home-in-the-suburbs.html).

7. See Eric Jacobsen, *Sidewalks in the Kingdom: New Urbanism and the
Christian Faith* (Grand Rapids: Brazos, 2003), 43.

8. See, for example, Roberto A. Ferdman, "Stop Eating So Much Meat, Top
U.S. Nutritional Panel Says," *Washington Post*, February 19, 2015, https://www.
washingtonpost.com/news/wonk/wp/2015/02/19/eating-a-lot-of-meat-is-hurtin
g-the-environment-and-you-should-stop-top-u-s-nutritional-panel-says.

9. Ronald Sider in *Rich Christians in an Age of Hunger* (5th ed. [Nashville:
Thomas Nelson, 2005]) will ruin your banana-eating experience for keeps. Ever
thought about why the fruit—which is grown nowhere near Michigan—is so
cheap and readily available? Hint: someone's not getting his or her fair wage
(see pp. 175–77).

10. Barbara Kingsolver's *Animal, Vegetable, Miracle: A Year of Food Life* (New
York: Harper, 2007) chronicles her family's yearlong experiment in eating only
local food, including produce and animals they raised themselves. Each family
member got to pick one thing on which the whole family would splurge for the year:
one chose coffee, another bananas, and so on. A few other staples were allowed,
like flour and oil, but otherwise if it wasn't locally in season, it was off-limits.

Chapter 11 Unselfish Self-Care

1. Kathryn Greene-McCreight, *Darkness Is My Only Companion: A Christian Response to Mental Illness*, 2nd ed. (Grand Rapids: Brazos, 2015), 117.

2. Writes Kathleen Norris in *The Quotidian Mysteries: Laundry, Liturgy and
"Women's Work"* (Costa Mesa, CA: Paulist Press, 1998): "This may sound like
a simple thing, but it is not easy to maintain faith, hope, or love in the everyday.
I wonder if this is because human pride, and particularly a preoccupation with
intellectual, artistic or spiritual matters, can provide a convenient way to ignore
our ordinary, daily, bodily needs" (11).

3. Stanley Hauerwas, *The Peaceable Kingdom: A Primer in Christian Ethics*
(Notre Dame, IN: University of Notre Dame Press, 1983), 31.

4. Ibid.

5. Ibid., 8.

Chapter 12 Just Living

1. John M. Perkins, *Beyond Charity: The Call to Christian Community Development* (Grand Rapids: Baker, 1993), 28.

2. The irony of the white suburban myth is that my own neighborhood is a mix of people of many races and nationalities—black, white, Hispanic, Middle Eastern, Pacific Islander, African, Asian—but they rarely interact. It was only when Sam began attending a daycare three doors down from our house that we really connected in a daily, meaningful way with our neighbors who aren't white.

3. "The core claim of this book is that liturgies—whether 'sacred' or 'secular'—shape and constitute our identities by forming our most fundamental desires and our most basic attunement to the world. In short, liturgies make us certain kinds of people, and what defines us is what we *love*" (James K. A. Smith, *Desiring the Kingdom: Worship, Worldview, and Cultural Formation* [Grand Rapids: Baker Academic, 2009], 25).

4. See Scott Bader-Saye, *Following Jesus in a Culture of Fear* (Grand Rapids: Brazos, 2007), 16.

5. "Ethics is not about being clever in a crisis but about forming a character that does not realize it has been in a crisis until the 'crisis' is over" (Samuel Wells, *Improvisation: The Drama of Christian Ethics* [Grand Rapids: Brazos, 2004], 12).

6. This may be one of the reasons why new monastics have struggled—as Tim Otto pointed out to us when reading the early drafts of this book—to attract people of color in shared communal life. A bunch of white folks tell their black friends, "Hey guys, we're thinking that lament might be a good idea. Want to join us? Oh, and also, your hard-won middle-class dignity might endanger your soul: how does downward mobility sound?" This is overstating the case, obviously, but it explains some of the pushback I heard at Duke Divinity School from black students as they engaged new monasticism.

7. Also, when whites start lamenting, the black community gets understandably nervous: the focus is now on a white person, again; everyone now has to manage a white person's emotions, again. Historically speaking, the tears of white women in particular are a fear trigger; there could be consequences, meted out by the men who love them, upon those who made them cry. See Robin DiAngelo, "White Women's Tears and the Men Who Love Them," The Good Men Project, September 19, 2015, http://goodmenproject.com/featured-content/white-womens-tears-and-the-men-who-love-them-twlm/.

8. Our former housemate from Isaiah House, Rev. Hannah Bonner, is deeply invested in seeking justice for the family of Sandra Bland, the young black woman who was found hanging in her Waller County, Texas, jail cell after being arrested during a traffic stop.

9. Ronald J. Sider, *Just Politics: A Guide for Christian Engagement* (Grand Rapids: Brazos, 2012), 8–10.

222 Notes to Pages 193–210

10. Eric Lacy, "Lansing Keeps Doors Open for Refugees, Immigrants," *Lansing State Journal*, December 14, 2015, http://www.lansingstatejournal.com/story /news/local/2015/12/14/lansing-refugee-immigrant-resettlement/77299876/.

11. As noted above, Howard Thurman uses this language throughout *Jesus and the Disinherited* (1949; repr., Boston: Beacon, 1996).

12. Ongoing missions or practices of social justice at Sycamore Creek Church generally start with small groups, which then invite the larger congregation and even other churches and organizations to join. Otherwise our missional endeavors risk becoming sponsored by no one in particular, and no one shows up.

13. For instance, out of respect for Erin's mental health, Erin and Dave discerned that she would stop volunteering meals and time at the homeless shelter, for now.

14. Stanley Hauerwas, *The Peaceable Kingdom: A Primer in Christian Ethics* (Notre Dame, IN: University of Notre Dame Press, 1983), 150.

15. Perkins, *Beyond Charity*, 28.

Appendix C The Arthurs' Christmas Letter

1. Gary Chapman's *Five Love Languages* books—for marriage, parenting, and other relationships—are perennial best sellers.

2. Mike Slaughter, *Christmas Is Not Your Birthday: Experience the Joy of Living and Giving like Jesus* (Nashville: Abingdon, 2011).